CHHATTISGARH

A STATE STUDY GUIDE

DEEPAK KUMAR

Published by

Hawk Press
4836/24, Ansari Road, Daryaganj
New Delhi – 110 002
Phones: 91-11-23278618, 91-11-43667199
E-mail: thehawkpress@gmail.com
www.thehawkpress.com

ISBN: 978-93-88318-74-7

Preface

Chhattisgarh is one of the 29 states of India, located in the centre-east of the country. It is the tenth-largest state in India, with an area of 135,191 km (52,198 sq mi). With a population of 25.5 million, Chhattisgarh is the 17th-most populated state in the country. A resource-rich state, it is a source of electricity and steel for the country, accounting for 15% of the total steel produced. Chhattisgarh is one of the fastest-developing states in India.

The state was formed on 1 November 2000 by partitioning 10 Chhattisgarhi and 6 Gondi speaking southeastern districts of Madhya Pradesh. The capital city is Raipur. Chhattisgarh borders the states of Madhya Pradesh in the northwest, Uttar Pradesh in the north, Jharkhand in northeast, Maharashtra in the southwest, Telangana and Andhra Pradesh in the south, Odisha in the southeast. Currently the state comprises 27 districts.

The climate in Chhattisgarh is governed by a monsoon weather pattern. The distinct seasons are summer (March to May), winter (November to February), and the intervening rainy months of the southwest monsoon (June to September). The summer is hot, dry, and windy, with high temperatures typically reaching at least 85 °F (about 30 °C) in all parts of the state; in some areas temperatures regularly rise above 100 °F (upper 30s C). Winters are usually pleasant and dry, with high temperatures in the upper 70s F (mid-20s C). In December and January there is considerable rainfall over the northern part of the state, although the state as a whole receives most of its precipitation during the southwest monsoon. Rainfall usually ranges from 47 to 60 inches (1,200 to 1,500 mm) annually.

The economy of Chhattisgarh is founded primarily on mining, agriculture, energy production, and manufacturing. The state has major deposits of coal, iron ore, dolomite, and other minerals. The central lowland is known especially for its abundant rice production, and the state as a whole provides the bulk of the country's tendu leaves for bidis. Chhattisgarh also is a significant regional supplier of electricity, from both thermal and hydroelectric generators. The state's manufacturing activities focus largely on metals production.

The structure of Chhattisgarh's government, like that of most other Indian states, is defined by the national constitution of 1950. The head of state—the governor—is appointed by the president of India. The governor is aided and advised by a chief minister, who heads the Council of Ministers, which is responsible to the elected Legislative Assembly (Vidhan Sabha). Although the political capital of Chhattisgarh is Raipur, the High Court is located in Bilaspur. A chief justice presides over the High Court.

Local government includes several divisions, which are subdivided further into districts. Each division is administered by a commissioner, while each is headed by a collector. Collectors exercise both executive and magisterial power.

This is a reference book. All the matter is just compiled and edited in nature, taken from the various sources which are in public domain.

This book is endeavours to present before the readers a panoramic view of the state, its districts, places, cultures, arts and crafts, developmental policies, economy along with history of dynasties that ruled the state.

—Editor

ABOUT THE BOOK

Chhattisgarh, state of east-central India. It is bounded by the Indian states of Uttar Pradeshand Jharkhand to the north and northeast, Odisha (Orissa) to the east, Telangana (formerly part of Andhra Pradesh) to the south, and Maharashtra and Madhya Pradesh to the west. Its capital is Raipur. Area 52,199 square miles (135,194 square km). The state was formed on 1 November 2000 by partitioning 10 Chhattisgarhi and 6 Gondi speaking southeastern districts of Madhya Pradesh. The capital city is Raipur. Chhattisgarh borders the states of Madhya Pradesh in the northwest, Uttar Pradesh in the north, Jharkhand in northeast, Maharashtra in the southwest, Telangana and Andhra Pradesh in the south, Odisha in the southeast. Currently the state comprises 27 districts. The Government of Chhattisgarh also known as the State Government of Chhattisgarh, or locally as State Government, is the supreme governing authority of the Indian state of Chhattisgarh and its 27 districts. It consists of an executive, led by the Governor of Chhattisgarh, a judiciary and a legislative branch. The key political players in Chhattisgarh state in central India are the ruling Bharatiya Janata Party, Indian National Congress, Janta Congress Chhattisgarh and Bahujan Samaj Party. This book is endeavours to present before the readers a panoramic view of the state, its districts, places, cultures, arts and crafts, developmental policies, economy along with history of dynasties that ruled the state.

Contents

1

State at a Glance

Chhattisgarh is one of the 29 states of India, located in the centre-east of the country. It is the tenth-largest state in India, with an area of 135,191 km (52,198 sq mi). With a population of 25.5 million, Chhattisgarh is the 17th-most populated state in the country. A resource-rich state, it is a source of electricity and steel for the country, accounting for 15% of the total steel produced. Chhattisgarh is one of the fastest-developing states in India.

The state was formed on 1 November 2000 by partitioning 10 Chhattisgarhi and 6 Gondi speaking southeastern districts of Madhya Pradesh.

The capital city is Raipur. Chhattisgarh borders the states of Madhya Pradesh in the northwest, Uttar Pradesh in the north, Jharkhand in northeast, Maharashtra in the southwest, Telangana and Andhra Pradesh in the south, Odisha in the southeast.

Currently the state comprises 27 districts.

AT A GLANCE

Formed : November 1, 2000.

State Capital : Raipur

Area : 1,37,898 square kilometres (9th largest state in India).

Location : Central India, surrounded by six states – Andhra Pradesh, Maharashtra, Madhya Pradesh, Uttar Pradesh, Jharkhand and Orissa - Strategic Location.

Forest area : 43.35 percent. There are 3 national parks and 11 wildlife sanctuaries in the state - Rich in Bio-diversity.

Population : 25,540,000 (2011 Census).

Number of districts : 27

Population density : 185 persons per square Kilometres. (India average: 350). (Male/Female Ratio - 1000/991)

Literacy Rate : 71.04% (Female - 60.59%)

Climate : Tropical, with hot summers and cool winters.

Annual Rainfall : 1,800 millimeters

Rivers : Mahanadi is the main river, with Shivnath, Hasdeo, Kelo, Arpa as tributaries. Indrawati is another major river.

Road Length : 34,930 kilometres.

Rail Length : 1,108 Kilometres.

Airport : Raipur (with Night landing facilities).

Airstrips : Bhilai, Bilaspur, Korba, Raigarh, Jadgalpur, Ambikapur, Jashpurnagar and Sarangarh.

Languages : Hindi, Chhattisgarhi, Local dialects and English.

Time Zone : GMT + 5.30 hrs

National highways : 11 national highways (2,225 kms.). Good internal road network in the state, rapid improvement.

High court : Bilaspur

Labour Court and Industrial Disputes Trubunal : Raipur

ETYMOLOGY

There are several opinions as to the origin of the name *Chhattisgarh*, which in ancient times was known as Dakshina Kosala (South Kosala). "Chhattisgarh" was popularised later during the time of the Maratha Empire and was first used in an official document in 1795.

It is claimed that Chhattisgarh takes its name from the 36 ancient forts in the area. (*chhattis*—thirty-six, and *garh*—fort.) The old state had 36 demesnes (feudal territories): Ratanpur, Vijaypur, Kharound, Maro, Kautgarh, Nawagarh, Sondhi, Aukhar, Padarbhatta, Semriya, Champa, Lafa, Chhuri, Kenda, Matin, Aparora, Pendra, Kurkuti-kandri, Raipur, Patan, Simaga, Singarpur, Lavan, Omera, Durg, Saradha, Sirasa, Menhadi, Khallari, Sirpur, Figeswar, Rajim, Singhangarh, Suvarmar, Tenganagarh and Akaltara. However, experts do not agree with this explanation, as 36 forts cannot be archaeologically identified in this region.

Another view, more popular with experts and historians, is that Chhattisgarh is the corrupted form of *Chedisgarh* which means *Raj* or "Empire of the Chedis". In ancient times, Chhattisgarh region had been part of the Chedi dynasty of Kalinga, in modern Odisha. In the medieval period up to 1803, a major portion of present eastern Chhattisgarh was part of the Sambalpur Kingdom of Odisha.

ORIGIN

The name Chhattisgarh is not ancient and has come into popular usage in the last few centuries. In ancient times the region was called Dakshin Kosala. All inscription, literary works and the accounts of foreign travellers, call this region Kosala of Dakshin Kosala. According to Hari Thakur, the contest between Jabalpur and Chhattisgarh for the name Mahakosala is settled beyond doubt in favour of Chhattisgarh in the light of available evidence. Even during the reign of the Mughals, it was called Ratanpur territory and not Chhattisgarh. The word Chhattisgarh was popularized during the Maratha period and was first used in an official document in 1795.

A British Chronicler, J.B. Beglar provides and interesting story explaining the origins of the name Chhattisgarh. It becomes very relevant in the context of contemporary caste consciousness and the caste configuration of the region. According to Beglar "the real name is Chhattisghar and not Chhattisgarh. There is a tradition saying that ages ago about the time of Jarasandha, thirty six families of dalits (leather workers) emigrated southwards from Jarasandha's kingdom and established themselves in country, which after them is called Chhattisgarh".

Another common explanation regarding the origins of the name Chhattisgarh is that it denotes the number of forts in the region, which are supposed to be thirty six in number. However, experts do not agree with this explanation, as thirty-six forts cannot be identified in the region. An explanation popular with the experts and historians in that Chhattisgarh is the corrupted form of 'Chedisgarh' or the political seat of the Chedis.

Recent Events: On September 3, 2005, twenty policemen were killed by a mine in the district of Bijapur. The mine had been laid there by Naxalite rebels, who have joined with the rebels in Nepal. (20 indische Polizisten durch Mine getotet, September 4, 2005, Neue Zurcher Zeitung).

On February 28, 2006, 55 civilians were killed in Dantewada District after their trucks were blown up by Naxalites, one of the deadliest such Naxalite attacks in India's history. Smaller numbers of people have continued to perish in continued attacks related to the Naxalite rebellion. (Fear triggers exodus in India's Maoist Badlands, March 8, 2006, ABC News).

On March 25, 2006, thirteen civilians were killed in Kanker District after a land mine detonated underneath their jeep. Naxalite rebel involvement has been alleged by local police. (India landmine blast 'kills 13', March 25, 2006, BBC News).

On April 28, 2006, thirteen out of a group of fifty hostages were found partly beheaded in Dantewada District. Naxalite rebels are suspected in the hostage-taking and the massacre. (India rebels 'kill 13 villagers', April 28, 2006, BBC News).

Recently a law has been passed requiring conversion from one religion to another to be notified to the authorities 30 days beforehand. Citizens who fail to do this can face up to a year in jail. According to the BBC `conversion is a major political issue in the state`

Economy: Chhattisgarh's gross state domestic product for 2004 is estimated at 12 billion USD in current prices. After partition, this mineral-rich state produces 30% of the output of the old Madhya Pradesh state.

The state's economy is further fuelled by the presence of the Bhilai Steel Plant, S.E.C.Railway Zone, BALCO Aluminium Plant (Korba), and NTPC Korba (National Thermal Power Corporation Ltd.) and S.E. Coal Ltd. The city of Korba is a hub for power generation, from where the electricity is supplied to several other Indian states. Serious shortage of electric power makes Chattisgarh towns in summer less livable. Chattisgarh's southern area consists of high iron ore available where NMDC is excavating to meet the iron demand in India and as well sending to countries like Japan. NMDC is located in dantewara district. Recently ESSAR has started transporting iron ore through pipe lines to vizag.

The state is also launching an ambitious plan to become biofuel self-sufficient by 2015 by planting crops of jatropha.

According to a mythological legend, Ram, during his Vanvas stayed in Dakshin Kosala. Which is modern day Chhattisgarh. The unbroken history of Chhattisgarh or of South Kosala can be traced back to fourth century AD and its mythological history goes back as far back as the Mahabharata and the Ramayana. About the history of the region the famous historian C.W. Wills writes, 'in the 10th century AD a powerful Rajput family ruled at Tripuri near Jabalpur, Issuing from this kingdom of Chedi (also known as Kalchuri dynasty) a scion of the royal house by the name Kalingraja, settled about the year 1000 AD, at Tuman, a site at present marked only by a few ruins in the north east of the erstwhile Laphazamidari of The Bilaspur district. His grandson Ratanraja founded Ratanpur Which continued as the capital of a large part of the country now known as Chhattisgarh. This Rajput family called themselves the Haihaya dynasty. This dynasty continued ruling Chhattisgarh for six centuries about the 14th century it split into parts, the elder branch continued at Ratanpur, while the younger settled in semi-independent state at Raipur. At the end of 16th century it acknowledged the suzerainty of the Mughals, In Bastar, in the middle ages, Chalukya dynasty established its rule. The first Chalukya ruler was Annmdev, who established the dynasty in Bastar in 1320.

The Marathas attacked Chhattisgarh in 1741 and destroyed the Haihaya power. In 1745 AD after conquering the region, they deposed Raghunathsinghji, the last surviving member of the Ratanpur house. In 1758, the Maraths finally annexed Chhattisgarh, it came directly under Maratha rule and Bimbaji Bhonsle, was appointed the rule. After death of Bimbaji Bhonsle, the Marathas adopted the Suba system. The Maratha rule was a period of unrest and misrule. There was large-scale loot and plunder by the Maratha army. The Maratha officials were openly surrendering the interests of the region to the British. As a result of this, the region became extremely poor and the people began resenting the Maratha rule. Only the Gonds continued to resist and challenge the advances of the Marathas and this led to several conflicts and much animosity between the Gonds and the Marathas (Captain Blunt, 1975). The Pindaris also attacked and plundered the region in the beginning of the Nineteenth Century.

In 1818 Chhattisgarh came under some sort of British control for the first time. In 1854, when the province of Nagpur lapsed to the British government, Chhattisgarh was formed into a deputy commissionership with its headquarters at Raipur. Historian C.W. Wills, writing about Chhattisgarh says, Chhattisgarh presents the remarkable picture of a Hindu government continuing till modern times outside the sphere of direct Mohammedan control. The British made certain changes in the administrative and revenue systems of Chhattisgarh, which adversely affected the people of Chhattisgarh. The intrusion of the British was resisted strongly in Bastar by the tribals and the Halba rebellion which lasted nearly five year (1774-1779) was the first documented rebellion against the British and Marathas in Bastar.

The First war of independence in 1857 was spearheaded in

Chhattisgarh by Vir Narain Singh who was a benevolent jamindar of Sonakhan. The British arrested him in 1856 for looting a trader's grain stocks and distributing it amongst the poor in a severe famine year. In 1857 with the help of the solders of the British Army at Raipur, Vir Narain Singh escaped form prison. He reached Sonakhan and formed an army of 500 men. Under the leadership of Smith, a powerful British army was dispatched to crush the Sonakhan army. The British succeeded after a prolonged battle and Vir Narain Singh was arrested and later hanged on the 10th December, 1857. He became the first martyr from Chhattisgarh in the War of Independence. Vir Narain Singh's martyrdom has been resurrected in the 1980's and he has become a potent symbol of Chhattisgarhi pride.

HISTORY

Ancient and medieval history

In ancient times, this region was known as Dakshina Kosala. This area also finds mention in Ramayana and Mahabharata. Between the sixth and twelfth centuries, Sharabhpurias, Panduvanshis (of Mekala and Dakshina Kosala), Somavanshi, Kalachuri and Nagavanshi rulers dominated this region. The Bastar region of Chhattisgarh was invaded by Rajendra Chola I and Kulothunga Chola I of the Chola dynasty in the 11th century.

Colonial and post-independence history

Chhattisgarh was under Maratha rule (Bhonsales of Nagpur) from 1741 to 1845 AD. It came under British rule from 1845 to 1947 as the Chhattisgarh Division of the Central Provinces. Raipur gained prominence over the capital Ratanpur with the advent of the British in 1845. In 1905, the Sambalpur district was transferred to Odisha and the estates of Surguja were transferred from Bengal to Chhattisgarh.

The area constituting the new state merged into Madhya Pradesh on 1 November 1956, under the States Reorganisation Act, 1956 and remained a part of that state for 44 years. Prior to its becoming a part of the new state of Madhya Pradesh, the region was part of old Madhya Pradesh State, with its capital at Bhopal. Prior to that, the region was part of the Central Provinces and Berar (CP and Berar) under the British rule. Some areas constituting the Chhattisgarh state were princely states under the British rule, but later on were merged into Madhya Pradesh.

Separation of Chhattisgarh

Mantralaya in Naya (New) Raipur

The present state of Chhattisgarh was carved out of Madhya Pradesh on 1 November 2000. The demand for a separate state was first raised in the 1920s. Similar demands kept cropping up at regular intervals; however, a well-organised movement was never launched. Several all-party platforms were formed and they usually resolved around petitions, public meetings, seminars, rallies and strikes. A demand for separate Chhattisgarh was raised in 1924 by the Raipur Congress unit and also discussed in the Annual Session of the Indian Congress at Tripuri. A discussion also took place of forming a Regional

Congress organisation for Chhattisgarh. When the State Reorganisation Commission was set up in 1954, the demand for a separate Chhattisgarh was put forward, but was not accepted. In 1955, a demand for a separate state was raised in the Nagpur assembly of the then state of Madhya Bharat.

The 1990s saw more activity for a demand for the new state, such as the formation of a statewide political forum, especially the Chhattisgarh Rajya Nirman Manch. Chandulal Chadrakar led this forum, several successful region-wide strikes and rallies were organised under the banner of the forum, all of which were supported by major political parties, including the Indian National Congress and the Bharatiya Janata Party.

The new National Democratic Alliance (NDA) government sent the redrafted Separate Chhattisgarh Bill for the approval of the Madhya Pradesh Assembly, where it was once again unanimously approved and then it was tabled in the Lok Sabha. This bill for a separate Chhattisgarh was passed in the Lok Sabha and the Rajya Sabha, paving the way for the creation of a separate state of Chhattisgarh. The President of India gave his consent to the Madhya Pradesh Reorganisation Act 2000 on 25 August 2000. The Government of India subsequently set 1 November 2000, as the day the state of Madhya Pradesh would be divided into Chhattisgarh and Madhya Pradesh.

TRIBAL PROTESTS AND REBELLIONS

Chhattisgarh is generally perceived as a tribal dominated state. Although this is factually incorrect it does reflect the significantly high proportion of tribals in the region. It also underscores a fundamentally important point that the tribals in Chhattisgarh have been able to retain their culture and traditional way of life despite the all pervasive influence of forces of modernity. While tribal people constitute 7.8% and 23% of the total population of India and Madhya Pradesh respectively they constitute 32.5 % of the population of Chhattisgarh. According to the 1991 census the tribal population in the then districts of Chhattisgarh was Durg –12.6 %, Raipur–18.6%, Rajnandgaon –25.3 %, Bilaspur -23.4 % Surguja –54.8%,

Raigarh –45.5%, Bastar –67.7 %. The various tribes in the Chhattisgarh region are Gonds, Muria, Bhumja, Baiga, Kanars, Kawars, Halbas etc. A few of these tribes particularly the Gonds have influenced by the Hindu tradition and have in turn influenced local practices in the Hindu tradition as well. Other tribes like the Kamars and the Baigas have largely been untouched by the mainstream and have retained more of their traditional culture and way of life.

Chhattisgarh has withnessed several tribal rebellions starting from the late 18 century through the 19 century to the first few decades of the 20 century. Some of these tribal revolts were localised while others were more widespread. Geographically too, the rebellions were not centred in one region, in some of them precipitating factors were immediate and local in nature and in some the revolt took its time to brew.

However the central narrative of these rebellions remained largely common and unchanged. All these rebellions were focused and asserted the traditionally inalienable right of the tribals on the local resources land and forests. Often the mobilisation was around the issues of tradition culture and the tribal way of life.

These rebellions were also protest against an alien system of governance and an alien political, economic and social order that had been forced upon them by the British. These tribal rebellions, although they predominantly took place in Bastar were spread across the various tribal areas of Chhattisgarh as well. The assimilation of this tradition of protest and rebellion by the tribals will be critical in any attempt to forge a Chhattisgarh identify and for evolving a vibrant and inclusive Chhattisgarh ethos. An understanding of these rebellions and integrating them in the new Chhattisgarh ethos will contribute to the future and the success of the new state. In this section we shall briefly discuss the tribal rebellions of Chhattisgarh. The key tribal rebellions are listed:

1. Halba rebellion (1774-79)
2. Bhopalpatnam Struggle (1795)

3. Paralkot rebellion (1825)
4. Tarapur rebellion (1842-54)
5. Maria rebellion (1842-63)
6. First Freedom Struggle (1856-57)
7. Koi revolt (1859)
8. Muria rebellion (1876)
9. Rani rebellion (1878-82)
10. Bhumkal (1910)

The Halba rebellion is a very important event in the history of Bastar as it was responsible for the decline of the Chalukya dynasty, which in turn created circumstances that first brought the Marathas and then the British to the region. The rebellion was initiated in 1774 by the governor of Dongar, Ajmer Singh with the intention of establishing an independent kingdom at Dongar. The Halba tribe and Halba soldiers supported him. However, the fundamental reasons for the rebellion were economic in nature.

There had been a prolonged famine, which had severely affected the people who had very little cultivable land. The presence of Maratha forces and the terror caused by the East India Company in these adverse circumstances precipitated the rebellion. The stronger armies of Bastar supported by the British and the Marathas crushed the rebellion. A massacre of Halba tribesmen followed the defeat of the Halba army. However, the revolt created conditions for the decline of the Chalukya dynasty which in turn significantly altered the history of Bastar.

The Paralkot rebellion was representative of the resentment felt by the Abujhmarias against the invasion of outsiders, primarily the Marathas and the British. This rebellion was supported by the Abujhmarias and was led by Gend Singh a fellow Abhujmaria.

One of the objectives of the rebellion was to establish a world free of loot, plunder and exploitation. The presence of the Marathas and the British threatened the identity of the Abujmarias and they resisted this through organising the rebellion of Paralkot in 1825. The rebels were opposing the taxes levied by the Maratha rulers. In essence this rebellion was directed against the foreign interference and control of Bastar and wanted to re-establish the freedom of Bastar.

The rebellion of Tarapur (1842-54) was once again the assertion of the tribals against the invasion of their local culture and the tampering with their traditional principles of social, economic and political organization. It started with an opposition to taxes levied under the pressure of Anglo-Maratha rule. For the tribals, these experiences of coercive taxation were alien and new, and therefore they opposed them. The local Diwan became a symbol of oppression and bore the brunt of tribal anger.

The Maria rebellion, which lasted nearly 20 years from 1842 to 1863, was seemingly in favour of an inhuman practice of human sacrifice. In reality the revolt was against the insensitive and intrusive handling of tribal faith. The Anglo Maratha combine did not hesitate to enter and pollute the temple of Danteswari. The facts clearly indicate that this rebellion was more defensive in nature and was waged by the tribals to protect their land and tradition.

Furer Hamendorf (Aboriginal Rebellions in the Deccan, Man in India, No.4,1945, PP 2089) writes all these rebellions were defensive movements, they were the last resort of tribesmen driven to despair by the encroachments of outsiders on their land and economic resources What is surprising is not the occurrence of uprisings, but the infrequency of violent reaction on the part of the aboriginals to the loss of their ancestral lands and to their economic enslavement. Hutton extends the analysis and writes (as quoted in H.L. Shukla, Baster Ka Mukti Sangram, p 118) early days of British administration did great detriment to the economic position of tribes through ignorance and neglect of their right and customs.

Bastar was also actively involved in the First War of Independence of 1857 with Southern Bastar as the centre of the revolt. Under the leadership of Dhruvarao a battle was waged against the British. He belonged to one of the Maria tribes called Dorlaon and was supported by his tribesmen.

Later in 1858, the Gonds challenged the British in several battles. In 1859 a very important rebellion began to take shape in Southern Bastar with the tribals refusing to let contractors undertake cutting of Sal trees. The people of these Jamindaris were called Kois. This rebellion was against the decision of the British to give contracts for cutting forests to contractors from Hyderabad.

These contractors were also responsible for the exploitation of the tribals. The local tribals in 1859 decided that they would not allow the felling of a single tree. The British took this as a challenge to the might of the empire and used coercive methods to continue the felling of trees. This rebellion was loud and clear assertion by the tribals of their inalienable rights of the tribals on their forests and natural resources.

In 1867, Gopinath Kapardas was appointed the Diwan of Bastar State and was responsible for large scale exploitation of the tribal population. Tribals from different parganas jointly requested the King to remove the Diwan but the King did not concede to these demands. This led to the Muria Revolt of 1876 The rebelling tribals surrounded Jagdalpur on 2 March 1876; the King with great difficulty was able to inform the British forces. Finally a strong British army sent by the Resident of Orissa, crushed the rebellion.

SOCIAL STRUCTURE AND CONFIGURATION

Women in Chhattisgarh have traditionally enjoyed a kind of freedom denied to women elsewhere in the country. This position of women continues to be very much the same even in modern times. This comes out strongly from available data and from the general Development index in the Human Development Report (1998) of the Government of Madhya Pradesh. The districts of Chhattisgarh fare much better and rank higher in the Gender Development Index than most other districts of Madhya Pradesh. The relative freedom to women is evident in the local traditions and customs. The Pardah system, present in one form or the other in many parts of India is not present in Chhattisgarh except in a few Brahmin and Bania Communities.

According to another local custom, women, other than those of these caste can choose to terminate a marriage relationship and through a custom called Chudi pahanana, it she so desires. However, a mention of these progressive local customs, in no way suggests that the ideology of female subservience does not exist in Chhattisgarh. On the contrary, in spite of this male authority and dominance is seen quite clearly in the social and cultural life of Chhattisgarh.

The population of Chhattisgarh is notable for the high proportion of Scheduled Tribes and for specific Sects primarily constituted of Schedule Castes. Of the total population of Chhattisgarh, tribals constitute at least 32.5%, which is a significantly high percentage. In the last few decades, the demographic profile of tribal dominated areas has undergone a change. This is a cause for concern as it represents large-scale intrusion of non tribals in tribal areas.

This changing demographic profile is strongly evident in Bastar, where the proportion of tribals has decreased in the last few decades. The tribal areas of Chhattisgarh have witnessed several rebellions starting from 1774 onwards against the intrusion by outsiders, primarily the British, in the domain of traditional rights and the tribal way of life. Interestingly, since the 17th century, the social history of the non-tribal areas of Chhattisgarh has been marked by reform movements such as the Satnam sect. Kabir Panthis and the Movements of share croppers and agricultural labour.

Despite presence of a high tribal population and religious reform movements, the region is also the domain of classic Hindu culture (although in some rituals the impact of tribal rituals can be identified), in which the cult of Ram assumes an essential and central role. Impact of this domination in evident and has its manifestations in the growth of sectarian formations is contemporary politics.

In India, the combined population of the Scheduled Castes and Tribes is 23.6% of the total population and for Madhya Pradesh; this figure rises to 37.1%. The combined population of Scheduled Castes and Tribes in Chhattisgarh is significantly higher at 44.7% and this is largely due to a high proportion of tribal population, Although the Scheduled Castes do not constitute a very high proportion of the total population they are critical for understanding the social history of Chhattisgarh, which has been deeply influenced and effected by the religious reform movements.

THE MOVEMENT OF PRATHAK

The demand for a separate Chhattisgarh state was first raised in the early twenties. Similar demands kept cropping up at regular intervals; however, a well-organised movement was never launched. Several efforts were made by individuals and organisations towards highlighting the Chhattisgarh identity and expressing the sense of perceived marginalisation. There were certain protests with mass support but these were limited and sporadic. There were several all-party platforms formed and they usually resolved around petitions, public meetings, seminars, rallies and bandhs.

A demand for separate Chhattisgarh was raised in 1924 by the Raipur Congress unit, and later on also discussed in the Annual Session of the Indian Congress at Tripuri. A discussion also took place of forming a Regional Congress organisation for Chhattisgarh. Sporadic attempts to give a call for a separate state for Chhattisgarh continued in the years immediately following Independence. In 1955, a demand for a separate state was raised in the Nagpur assembly of the then state of Madhya Bharat.

When the State Reorganisation Commission was set up in 1954, the demand for a separate Chhattisgarh was put forward to it, through this was not accepted. It was reported that the State Reorganisation Commission rejected the demand for Chhattisgarh on the grounds that the prosperity of Chhattisgarh would compensate for the poverty of other regions of Madhya Pradesh.

The eighties were a comparatively quiet phase in the demand for Chhattisgarh. The 1990's saw more activity for a demand for the new state, such as formation of a state wide political forum, especially the Chhattisgarh Rajya Nirman Manch. The Late Chadulal Chadrakar led this forum, several successful region-wide Bandhs and rallies were organised under the banner of the forum all of which were supported by major political parties including the Congress and the BJP. The rallies of the all party forum were attended by leaders from most political parties.

THE CREATION

The Congress Government of Madhya Pradesh took the first institutional and legislative initiative for the creation of Chhattisgarh. On the 18 of March 1994, a resolution demanding a separate Chhattisgarh was tabled and unanimously approved by the Madhya Pradesh Vidhan Sabha. Both the Congress and the Bhartiya Janta Party supported the resolution.

The election manifestos of the Congress and the BJP for both the 1998 and the 1999 parliamentary elections as well as the Madhya Pradesh assembly election of 1998 included the demand for creation of separate Chhattisgarh. In 1998, the BJP led Union Government drafted a bill for the creation of a separate state of Chhattisgarh from sixteen districts of Madhya Pradesh. This draft bill was sent to the Madhya Pradesh assembly for approval. It was unanimously approved in 1998, although with certain modifications.

The union government did not survive and fresh elections were declared. The new National Democratic Alliance (NDA) government sent the redrafted Separate Chhattisgarh Bill for the approval of the Madhya Pradesh Assembly, where it was once again unanimously approved and then it was tabled in the Lok Sabha. This bill for a separate Chhattisgarh was passed in the Lok Sabha and the Rajya Sabha, paving the way for the creation of a separate state of Chhattisgarh. The President of India gave his consent to The Madhya Pradesh Reorganisation Act 2000 on the 25 of August 2000. The Government of India subsequently set the First day of November 2000 as the day on which the state of Madhya Pradesh would be bifurcated into Chhattisgarh and Madhya Pradesh. Many political observers have commented on the relatively peaceful manner in which the Chhattisgarh state has been created.

There is no single factor responsible for the creation of Chhattisgarh. It is in fact a complex interplay of a combination of factors that paved the path for a separate state. The long standing demand and the movement for Uttarakhand and Jharkhand which led to the acceptance of separate states for these two regions, created a sensitive environment for the Prithak Chhattisgarh demand. Therefore, the creation of Chhattisgarh coincided with the creation of these two states and became a concurrent process.

Another important factor leading to the creation of Chhattisgarh was that there was clear acceptance, within Chhattisgarh and outside that Chhattisgarh had a distinct socio-cultural regional identity that had evolved over centuries. A consensus had evolved and emerged on the distinctiveness of Chhattisgarh. The people of Chhattisgarh accepted this and saw Prithak Chhattisgarh as giving expression to this identity. A sense of relative deprivation had also developed in the region and people felt that a separate state was imperative for development to take place in the region. In a democratic polity, the people's demand has a high degree of legitimacy and weight. Therefore the people's demand voiced through democratic channels was heard and contributed immensely to the creation of Chhattisgarh.

The consensus regarding the distinctiveness of Chhattisgarh did not remain limited to its socio-cultural identity. All over Madhya Pradesh, the consensus on a need for separate Chhattisgarh was also carefully developed. This consensus cuts across geographical regions castes, classes and political parties. A strong reflection of this consensus was evident in the unanimous passing of the Chhattisgarh bill in the Madhya Pradesh Vidhan Sabha. This consensus is a pointer to the high degree of maturity of Madhya Pradesh polity and the smooth passage of the Prithak Chhattisgarh bill resulting in the peaceful and unanimous creation of a new state a tribute to this maturity.

SEED OF PROTEST AND CHANGE

Chhattisgarh primarily due to its large tribal population has historically not been a part of the mainstream and has therefore remained underdeveloped. Critical indicators for education and health have remained low. However, as stated above, the region was influenced by mainstream traditional Hindu culture as the overacting organising principle despite the presence of a large percentage of Scheduled Castes and Tribes.

This oppressive, hierarchical social and religious order was not accepted, and from the 17th century onwards, the social history of Chhattisgarh is marked by the process of questioning and protests in the form of a number of socio-religious reform movements. These movements established a tradition of protest and have played a critical role in creation of the identity of Chhattisgarh, Initiated by sects like the Satnam Panth, the kabirpanthis and the Raedasis spread over all over Chhattisgarh, they carried the message of equality. Often the spread of these movement was within the boundaries of Chhattisgarh and therefore these movements contributed indirectly towards creating a regional consciousness.

An illustrative case would be the Satnam Panth, which emerged as sectarian formation, primarily reconstituting a small number of dalit groups by incorporating them as Satnamis, The Satnam Panths was an attempt to negotiate and cope with the cultural and economic processes in Chhattisgarh in the nineteenth century. It was a new sect, formed primarily amongst the poors of Chhattisgarh in the second decade of the nineteenth century and was led by Ghasidas, a humble farm worker.

This community constituted a significant proportion, a little less then one sixth, of the total population of Chhattisgarh. They either owned land or were sharecroppers and farm workers. The new sect was given the name of Satnam and its followers were expected to believe only in the formless - Satnam or the true name. Gradually, the followers of this sect were given the name satnamis. Satnamis abstain from meat, liquor, tobacco, certain vegetables and red pulses. Satnam Panth rejected the deities and idols of the Hindu pantheon. The panth preaches a casteless order. Guru Ghasidas initiated a Guru parampara in the sect, which became hereditary. The main religious centres of the sect in Chhattisgarh are Bhandar and Girod.

In the nineteenth century a new system of property rights and revenue collection known as the malgujari settlement was introduced in Chhattisgarh. The new system was implemented with the sole purpose of expropriation and exploitation of marginal farmers, sharcropers and farm servants by the upper caste Malgujars. Satnam Panth and its followers responded to this exploitative system through various strategies. In several cases the Satnamis deserted villages or continued with the process of Lakhabatta or the periodic redistribution of land, despite the implementation of the new system. Their united challenge to the upper caste Malgujars over the issues of rent and loss of land in the last decade of the nineteenth century was a reflection of the solidarity of Satnamis. This form of protest and response to the new system or property rights and malgujari settlements was widespread among the Satnamis of Chhattisgarh.

The primary concern of the Anglo Maratha politics in the Nineteenth century was of expropriation and consolidation of power. Guru Ghasidas the founder of the Satmani sect realised this. He believed that the politics of the Anglo-Marathas was deprived of morality. He worked towards uniting all downtrodden persons to morally oppose the immoral politics of the British The people of Chhattisgarh realised the potential threat of the British and were terror struck by the exploitative nature of their policies. Despite this, they were unable to unite under one flag to oppose the British. It was at this juncture that Ghasidas made efforts to unite the people of Chhattisgarh through the ideology of equality and non-violence.

Other sects emerged in response to the hierarchical social

order and linked Chhattisgarh to other social reform movements in the country. However the regional specificities of these sects remained unaltered. Kabir Panthis for example, are largely recruited from dalits and have a substantial presence in Chhattisgarh. The followers of this sect adhere to the teachings and principles of Kabir, the revolutionary social reformer saint poet of the sixteenth century.

The centres of Kabir Panth activities are monasteries which are placed in the charge of Mahants. In Chhattisgarh, Kabir Panthi monasteries are in Kudurmal, Kharsia, Champa, Hardi, Bangoli, Banni, Dhamdha, Panda, Tarai and Ratanpur. The Kabir Panth does not believe in caste hierarchies. However in contemporary times the Panth has been divided along caste lines. The only time that they do not adhere to caste hierarchies is in the presence of the Chief Guru on the birth anniversary of Kabir. All who desire to become members of the Panth are required to renounce polytheism and to acknowledge their belief in only one god. The Kabir Panth of Chhattisgarh are descendents of Dharmadasa, one of the disciples of Kabir who established the Panth in Chhattisgarh. There fore the branch of the Kabir Panth in Chhattisgarh is also known as Dharmadasa or Bhai branch.

The Ramnami Panth is small sect in Chhattisgarh with a membership primarily from the dalit community. This sect propagates the cult of Rama among the dalits and does not believe in Brahmins as a medium for worshipping god. Ramnamis are found chiefly on the southern side of the Mahanadi in Chhattisgarh. This sect is easily distinguishable as they carry a flute and put peacock feathers around their caps. Ramnamis as the name suggests chant the name of Ram. They of ten get their bodies tattooed with the name of Ram.

The social religious reformer Ramananda had a committed dalit follower from Chhattisgarh. His name was Ravi Das or Rae Das. Gradually, the followers of Rae Das formed a separate sect and started calling themselves Rae Das Panthis or simply Raedasis. A striking similarity between all these sects is that the followers are drawn mostly from the Dalit communities.

Secondly all these sects spread the message of equality.

The most widespread and important rebellion was the Bhumkal rebellion of 1910 that spread to 46 of the 84 parganas of Bastar. The term Bhumkal is significant as it refers to the social solidarity of the members of a clan that binds them to each other and to their specific Bhumor land. The basic reasons listed for the Bhumkal rebellion by historians clearly reaffirms the findings from earlier rebellions.

It continued the tradition of tribal struggle for preserving and defending their traditions and their way of life and for reasserting their traditional rights on forests, land and natural resources. One of the main reasons for the rebellion is given by Standan dispossession of traditional forests and land resources had been the most important cause of the Bhumkal rebellion. In 1908, the forests were first made reserved forests and the contractors given rights to take timber and wood for railway sleepers.

This deprived the tribals of one of their main sources of their livelihood. Leasing out of liquor monopolies also aggravated the situation, as the locally made country liquor was declared illegal. The introduction of education and schools was seen by the tribals as an attempt by the State to subvert their culture and therefore became a precipitating factor. Finally, the brutality and exploitation by the police, which included begar by the officials culminated in the Bhumkal rebellion.

INTERVENTIONS

Reproductive Health: Socio-cultural determinants of women's health and nutrition have a cumulative effect over a life time and even across generations. To have adequate impact on reproductive health, the emphasis will have to shift from a narrow focus on maternal health to an entire "life cycle of the woman" approach and health issues of women must be seen as a subset of women's empowerment. Commitment to life cycle approach would include combating gender discrimination before birth in the form of sex selective abortion or pre-conception technologies. It would mean ensuring adequate access to all social services and opportunities for the girl child. It would mean adequate nutrition and life choices in adolescence, lack of discrimination in the institution of marriage and adequate access to good quality maternal care and protection from neglect and destitution in old age.

It also means an end to the various forms of violence against women. At all ages it implies that services accessed are gender sensitive and that there is special attention given to the entire range of reproductive health care including infertility management, access to a variety of contraceptives, prompt and effective care for reproductive tract infections. The government also recognises the urgency regarding promotion of sexual health, education regarding reproductive health issues and the need to ensure women's control over decision making with regard to their own bodies. In such a setting population stabilisation goals would be achieved. In its absence these goals would remain elusive.

For implementing these commitments, the Government would promote organisations and collective action by women, male and community participation on reproductive health issues, greater number of women health care providers and expanded facilities with convenient timings for women to access these. The build up of women's health committees and women health volunteers (Mitanins) in every hamlet expands enormously the ability of the government to strengthen these processes, and thereby fulfil its commitments.

Child Health

The Integrated Health and Population Policy recognises the rights of every child to adequate nutrition, to good health, to good quality education, to love and care and adult protection, as well as for opportunities for them to grow and attain their full potential.

For the pre- schoolchild, the Integrated Child Development Scheme (ICDS) will remain the key strategy. However, the current ICDS scheme would head to be strengthened into a comprehensive early childhood care programme with improvements in quality and outreach so that every pre-school child is assured of nutrition, pre school education and health care and every working mother is assured of day care support for young children.

Continuing efforts will be made to reduce child mortality to levels comparable to the best performing states of India. This would require prompt and adequate community and primary health care on the very first day of health need with adequate institutional referral support for the sick child. It would also require a considerable reduction in child malnutrition levels as well as preventive measures against epidemics and recurrent infections like diarrhoea, malaria and measles in young children. Every section of society, especially the local government bodies would be involved in this priority of accelerating child survival.

The Government also recognises that certain categories of children, like the handicapped child, children without adult protection, street children etc., have special health needs and would need to develop flexible partnership based approaches to address them.

Adolescent Health

The policy acknowledges the importance of providing information, guidance and counselling services to adolescents and orienting parents about needs, issues and constraints of adolescents.

The policy recognises that there is a need for further research to understand these issues. Adolescent health would be integrated into routine services. Specific programmes on adolescent nutrition, anaemia, reproductive health will be introduced along with good counselling and support systems to enable adolescents to reach their full potential. Mass screening and counselling would not only identify and immediately minimise anaemia ensured by iron deficiency, but it would also contribute to identifying sickle cell diseases and traits among adolescents leading to a reduction of the disease in the next generation.

Emphasis will also be put on skill and ability development

by the educational system keeping with the opportunities in the job market so as to enable youth to develop into responsible citizens with an abiding awareness of and adherence to secular principles and values enshrined in the Constitution of India. As regards sexual health and reproductive health issues priority would given to sharing adequate information and building adequate life skills in both men and women. This would be done by incorporating such issues into the formal education curriculum as well as non formal education and peer education approaches. The government recognises that population stabilisation goals like adequate spacing and delaying age of the women at marriage and at first birth as well as the goals of HIV/AIDS control programmes can be made only in a context where adolescents are fully informed and can make responsible choices on sexual and reproductive matters.

Communicable Diseases

An effective diseases surveillance system will be developed to monitor the magnitude and distribution of communicable diseases in different population groups. State and area specific plans and strategies will be developed and appropriate interventions will be identified incorporating new technological advances. All communicable disease control programmes will be integrated with each other and with the health system as a whole at the Gram Panchayat, Block and District levels to optimise use of resources and make programme implementation more effective.

The emphasis will be on prevention through appropriate evidence based, well monitored strategies. Prevention approaches would recognise centrality of community participation, intersectoral coordination and involvement of PRIs. Massive, well planned and focused BCC campaigns would also play a pivotal role. Current State priorities are will be the elimination of leprosy, polio, yaws and the reduction in vector borne diseases, tuberculosis and water borne and sanitation related diseases.

For effective control of malaria the key steps would be early diagnosis and prompt treatment of fever cases, active and passive surveillance through blood smear examination with quality laboratory diagnosis and reporting systems, locally planned and supportive vector control measures with special emphasis on bio-environmental methods, universal access to personal prophylaxis measures like pesticide impregnated bed nets, and early warning and effective response to disease outbreaks. For tuberculosis the key measures would be increased awareness of their roles amongst all health care providers, better communication with those affected by the disease, improved diagnostics integrated into all health care facilities, easy access to drugs at all times and good quality of follow up to ensure that the disease is treated adequately.

HIV/AIDS

The State will take pro-active steps to create public awareness regarding the emergence of HIV/AIDS as a major public health issue. One of the key strategies of prevention will be health education campaigns reaching out to all people - with an emphasis on adolescents, migrant workers and occupational or social sectors known to have high prevalence rates. Such reduction efforts would require the cooperation of a large number of community bound organisations and civil society groups. District based Voluntary Counselling and Testing Centres (VCTC) are established in all district hospitals and this would be extended to all referral centres. Treatment to reduce Trans Placental Transmission (Mother to Child Transmission) will be introduced. Home based care for People Living with HIV/AIDS (PLWHA) will be encouraged and supported.

There will be no discrimination in providing treatment to PLWHA in all public and private sector hospitals. Measures will be enforced to reduce transmission of HIV through blood transfusion and blood products. Strong advocacy and social mobilisation efforts will be made at all levels to promote collaboration between public, private and voluntary sector, all concerned departments and with citizen groups in responding to the pandemic of HIV/AIDS. The strategy to control HIV/

AIDS, Sexually Transmitted Infections (STI), Reproductive Tract Infections (RTI), Hepatisis B and Hepatisis C will be converged. The State will be sensitive and responsive to problems such as children with HIV/AIDS, orphaned children, abandoned patients, and legal issues arising out of the HIV pandemic.

Non-Communicable Diseases

Parallel to high levels of communicable diseases, the State is also witnessing a rising tide of noncommunicable disease, accounting for over forty percent of morbidity. This trend is likely to increase. The state recognises that a large part of non communicable disease morbidity and mortality can be prevented with effective primary health care strategies. One key strategy to address this would be to reduce the risk factors of non communicable diseases by using health education to promote healthier life style approaches.

It will initiate policies to discourage the use of tobacco and alcohol and addictive substances. Policies that would reduce consumption of these would include ban on direct and indirect advertising and sponsorship of sports and entertainment by manufacturers of tobacco and alcohol, higher taxation, sales to be permitted to persons only above the age of 25 years and sales to be barred within certain distance of educational institutions and sensitive areas. De-addiction strategies using group therapies will be supported besides individual therapy and counselling the role of exercise for those in sedentary occupations.

Reduced exposure to atmospheric pollutants, and reduced exposure to physical and mental stress would all be important components of life style changes needed. Diagnosis and treatment of non-communicable diseases will be made available at all levels with specialist care available at secondary referral (district) and tertiary care levels. At the primary care level medical officers would provide effective primary care based on standard treatment guidelines, and rational use of diagnostics and drugs.

Cancer management will be strengthened and facilities will be made available at regional levels. The State of Chhattisgarh will also plan responses to special challenges in non communicable health of which sickle cell disease is the most prevalent. A planned campaign against this disease should significantly reduce its prevalence in the next generation.

Mental Health

The State will make systematic and sustained efforts to enhance mental health services by improving training in psychiatry and psychology in medical and paramedical courses. The State will integrate psychiatric teams and services at district hospitals and plan for counselling services at Community Health Centres (CHCs). The State will introduce mental health component into school health services and support broad societal strategies to address violence particularly against women, and various forms of social discrimination, substance abuse and poverty that are underlying causes of poor mental health. The State will establish institutional mechanisms through which mental health services can be effectively and widely accessed.

Occupational Health and Disaster Management

The State will ensure occupational health standards for prevention of occupational health hazards in the organised sector as well as in the unorganised sector. There would be a state level unit entrusted with monitoring industries for adherence to health standards and ensuring that all employees are providing services for prompt recognition and management of occupational disease. Periodic health and disease surveys for occupational disease in disease prone settings like in coal mines would also be insisted upon. Disaster management units will be set up at the State and district levels to plan and coordinate rescue operations and control of outbreaks. The unit will ensure preparedness to deal with natural and man-made hazards and disasters and would ensure capacity building of the health functionaries responsible for health managements in disaster situations.

Elderly Health Care

With increasing age susceptibility to stress increases, chronic illnesses and disability becomes more prevalent, psychosocial crisis such as retirement, loss of income and loss of spouse become common. There is need for both community care and institutional care for the elderly. A number of resources potentially available to assist long term managed care of the elderly include old-age geriatric nursing homes, geriatric provisions in general nursing homes, day centres, and residential housing with provision for shared geriatric support including independent living units of the elderly. A comprehensive plan will be developed to provide holistic care for the elderly population. Health services for the elderly will be integrated with all health care services, with special geriatric health services available at the tertiary level. Raised public awareness of the needs and care of the elderly is also an important goal.

Disability

The State will adopt an inclusive approach for persons who are 'differently abled' with their full participation in decision making and implementation. The State will increase its role in respect to disability by way of prevention, early detection and intervention. The State will take appropriate measures to disseminate the Persons with Disabilities (Equal Opportunities, Protection of Rights and Full Participation) Act 1995. The State will promote universal immunisation, good nutrition, accident prevention etc. to prevent disabilities, ensure timely treatment at all levels, ensure access to rehabilitation services, access to aids and appliances and capacity building of health service providers to assist people with disabilities.

Urban Health

Chhattisgarh has a 20.09 % urban population. It is projected that the urban growth rate will be much higher than the rural growth rate in the coming decade. Urban areas would also be under pressure due to mass movement of migrants from rural areas both within the state and from poor areas of adjoining states. This has already led to the development of slums inhabited by an urban poor who lack access to any form of social security, whose access to social services is poor and whose living and working conditions make them even more vulnerable to ill health and disease than the rural poor.

The State will ensure basic amenities such as food security, safe drinking water, sanitation and education and healthcare facilities for the entire urban population, irrespective of their legal status.

The State will undertake mapping of urban slums with the help of municipal corporations and municipalities. The primary health care services for urban slum population will be strengthened with participation of public, private, urban self government bodies and of NGOs. Every 5000 urban population would have access to the preventive and promotive services of a trained public health nurse, assisted by community health volunteers and peer educators. Every 100,000 urban population would have access to an urban health care referral centre with adequate medical officers and basic health care. Specific health programmes would also reach out to all the marginalised and vulnerable sections comprising of the homeless, migrants, destitutes, mentally or physically challenged.

Emergency Health Services

The policy commits the state to strengthening and expanding emergency health services and trauma care to include accidents, emergency obstetric care and other surgical, medical and pediatric emergencies. The state will aim to achieve 24 hour access to Comprehensive Emergency Obstetric Services and other basic surgical services at CHC level (CHC is a well equipped 30 bedded basic hospitals) by the end of the twelfth plan period. Referral system with adequate transport and communication arrangements will be established to reduce time of access to emergency services from any habitation to one hour. Citizen's charter will assure emergency care for critical care in any hospital, public and private as determined by the Supreme Court of India.

Training of First Aid and Life Support Systems will be imparted to school, college and university students; teachers, factory workers, drivers, bus conductors and to all paramedicals. Special efforts will be made to enforce accident preventive measures such as protective gears in industry and safety belts in automobiles and use of helmets in two wheelers for personal safety.

AYUSH/ISM&H

Chhattisgarh being a tribal state with vast herbal diversity and wide range of ethno-traditional practices, the state policy recognises importance of AYUSH (Ayurveda, Yoga, Unani, Sidha, Homeo) system in addressing health needs.

Proper mapping of ethno traditional practices will be done in order to document them properly. Codification, standardisation and preservation of the natural resource practices of traditional healers and the natural resource base that these depend on would be initiated so as to help mainstream their knowledge into health systems. There shall also be adequate measures to find out and to address the gaps in existing practices of these systems as to improve them. All possible steps would be assured to promote only validated practices. The gaps between the various systems in terms of epistemology and understanding would be narrowed through research and development and through sharing information between the systems. The world of knowledge regarding these systems shall be kept open and effective linkages would be established with expert institutions and individuals of the arena within and outside the State towards expanding the available resources and capacities.

The State shall hence mainstream these systems of medicines for contributing to better health care to all. All the health care seekers shall be provided with an option of which system to choose from. Qualified practitioners of AYUSH systems shall be posted in mainstream health facilities to achieve this. The State will also provide training and orientation in respect to primary health care for institutionally qualified AYUSH practitioners and utilise their services to fill gaps in manpower at appropriate levels in the mainstream health facilities. Participation and proper role of AYUSH practitioners will be ensured in all national and state health programmes.

Community participation in AYUSH programmes and AYUSH content in BCC and community level health processes would be used to promote a holistic understanding of health and disease. AYUSH would then become a major contribution to preventive and promotive health care. Necessary budget allocation and resource support shall be ensured so as to fulfil the development needs in this arena.

Health Planning and Management

Health planning would ensure that the health system has a clear sense of direction and priorities, makes efficient use of resources and is responsive to peoples needs. Health planning would be ensured at the state level, district level, Janpad Panchayat level and Gram Panchayat level. At the Gram Panchayat and Janpad Panchayat level, indicators of health and related sectors measured in a participatory way and published, would guide planning. The statutory health committee of the panchayat (may be synonymous with district health societies at the district level) would be the main centre of planning of the health department, with civil society and community based organisations contributing.

At district level, planning would involve aggregation of Gram Panchayat and block plans along with inputs on disease profiles from epidemiological studies and disease surveillance systems, and inputs on service delivery from health management information systems. Feedbacks from the community and external evaluation studies would also contribute. District level planning would plan for raising adequate resources especially from budgetary support, for efficient use of resources and resource allocation to identified priorities, for human resource development, for efficient stock and inventory management and for coordination and convergence with all related sectors. District health planning would be done with participation of all concerned stakeholders in a district level health committee and would be provided with the highest quality of technical assistance.

State level health planning will largely be an aggregation of district plans. In addition to this State level health plans would address the area of medical education and health human resource development, will set and monitor quality standards and norms and lead on research and development issues. It will also ensure that equity concerns are addressed and uneven development within and across districts is corrected through appropriate resource allocation and technical support options. State health planning would also identify the technical resources required from the national and international levels, to meet the health needs of the people.

Implementation of the plans will depend on four crucial aspects of good governance:

A. Institutional separation of all procurement and civil works development aspects with transparent and efficient processes for these aspects which are subject to periodic public scrutiny.

B. Supportive workforce management policies.

C. Fair and merit cum seniority based choice of management leadership with assured tenures and periodic assessments of performance.

D. Professionalisation of management at all levels.

A commitment to professional management is a commitment to ensuring that all health management personnel at state and district levels have appropriate health management skills and qualification. It also implies that where required, management expertise and functions can be sought from or outsourced to external agencies. A corollary of this is a commitment to developing public health management and hospital administration training institutions in the State and ensuring that such institutions access the best talents nationally and internationally and use these talents to improve existing State level capacities.

Both health planning and health management would require appropriate institutional frameworks. The State and district health societies would play the key role in planning and monitoring, as well as coordinate between the training institutions, the technical assistance agencies, the health management information system and disease surveillance systems, and the autonomous arrangement made for infrastructure development, procurement of drugs and supplies and for overseeing logistics.

The State and district level leaderships within the directorate at the State level and the chief medical and health officer's office at the district level would act as the main implementation mechanism to which the staff and facilities shall report.

Technical assistance agencies would be encouraged and facilitated at State levels to act as additional technical capacity to the State and district health societies. The State Health Resource Centre, Regional Resource Centre, UNICEF, and technical assistance agencies of development partners would be supported to play this role. Suitable NGOs with health expertise who are active in the State would also be requested and supported to provide technical assistance in areas of their expertise.

Health Human Resource Development: The State will promote policies and institutions that ensure that the state generates health care professionals that it needs. It recognises that at the time of adoption of this policy there is a large vacancy situation, worst in the areas of specialists, but extending to medical officers, nurses, midwives and many categories of technical support staff. And with increasing needs and growth of this sector these human resource requirements would multiply. State planning would therefore rest on estimating future health human resource requirements and encouraging a mix of government and private sector institutions to create this human resource. A clear definition of quality norms and close monitoring and support to ensure that institutions maintain these would also be an element of State planning on health professional education.

In each technical and professional domain the State would have at least one or two institutions of international standards, equivalent to the best in the nation and with the ability to undertake research and development in their domain. Care would be taken to ensure that professional education prepares professionals with the knowledge, skills and attitudes necessary to serve Chhattisgarh's population, especially those living in rural areas and the most vulnerable sectors. The process of recruitment of both faculty and students to such institutions would also be tailored to achieve these outcomes. The State would also make a variety of skill upgradation options available for the medical professional in view of the lake of in specialists and the limitations of conventional strategies to close this gap within decades.

In addition to the above pre service training/education plans the State has adopted an in-service HRD policy that provides for periodic retraining and skill upgradation of all its personnel through a hierarchy of training institutions at state, regional and district level. Management training for all the public health sector staff in health management roles is a major component of this policy. Implementation of this in-service HRD policy would be a key to effective service delivery. The apex training institute in charge of all in service training and also playing the role of a policy planning institution for HRD would be the State Institute of Health and Family Welfare. A mandatory continuing medical education programme for all medical professionals would also be organised.

Health Financing: The State would ensure adequacy of funding in relation to the present and future needs and to the functions and responsibilities of the Department of Health and Family Welfare. The State will ensure increase in public heath sector allocation to 6% of the State budgetary allocation. The investments in primary, secondary and tertiary care and the ratio of expenditure between rural and urban areas will be based on the norms that will be developed regarding scale of services in these sectors. Resource flows will be managed so as to increase health facilities in the rural areas and increase resources available to vulnerable sectors.

The health budget would clearly define allocations district wise and such allocation would be in accordance with district health plans. District health planners would be aware of the resource envelope available to the district, the norms for inter-sectoral distribution, the proportions earmarked for mandatory spending items to reflect State planning priorities and the untied fund pool—so that genuine decentralisation is enabled. Delegation of financial resources and process to districts would be strengthened as parts of State Finance Commission recommendations for more effective decentralisation to PRIs in both rural and urban areas.

Recognizing that fund requirements are enormous, supplemental resource mobilisation options through donor support to hospital management committees and district health societies would be encouraged. Private sector investment for contribution to public health would also be encouraged where access to poor and quality and rate control are ensured. Recognising that the major part of total health expenditure, and therefore of health financing Chhattisgarh is not budgetary support but out of pocket household expenditure, the State shall endeavour to promote social security options that reduce the adverse impact of such household expenditure on levels of poverty and indebtedness.

Access and Rational Use of Drugs: The State is committed to the concept of access to essential drugs as a basic human entitlement. Chhattisgarh State will ensure annual increase of budgetary allocation for purchasing drugs and supplies for both in-patients and out-patients in the public health sector so as to keep abreast of increased utilisation of services and ensure that the poor have access to all essential and life saving drugs. Procurement of drugs will be transparent and efficient so as to ensure the most competitive costs, the best quality and no interruption in supply.

An essential drug list will be prepared and periodically updated for primary, secondary and tertiary hospitals. Rational use of drugs in the public sector, as defined by the essential drug list, is essential to keep the drug budget at affordable levels. Appropriate institutional framework for procurement of drugs and distribution of drugs will be put in place. Warehouses for drugs and supplies will be constructed and storage space of adequate standards will be created in all health institutions. Health staff will be trained in logistics management. Promotion of rational use of drugs in both public and in the private sector will reduce total expenditure on drugs and save patients from avoidable and adverse effects of improper and over use of drugs.

In line with a State drug policy the State would ensure registration of all drugs in the market with adequate information to both consumers and to those prescribing drugs. Hazardous and banned drugs will not be allowed in to the market and irrational drugs will be progressively weeded out. Regulation of prices and maintenance of quality standards would be ensured in coordination with Central Government institutions. Spurious drugs would be promptly uncovered and its producers and distributors given exemplary punishment.

Population Stabilisation: The State recognises that population stabilisation requires social development measures like better education; improved access to quality of health services, better nutrition, good employment opportunity, higher earnings, and social security-all contributing to improving quality of life.

In addition to the above objectives, the State will promote the ability of the family to be able to choose and plan consciously when and how many children it wants to have. Family Planning Services will not adopt coercive strategies in any form. The State recognises the importance of family planning services being made a part of life cycle approach to reproductive health and of comprehensive primary health care strategies. Good quality family welfare services and contraceptive technologies that are safe and effective will be promoted.

There will be promotion of use of safe, universally accessible temporary methods to delay the age of mother concerning her first child, to 21 years and ensure at least four years spacing between two children. Male responsibility in contraception as well as in all aspects of women's health care will be advocated to reduce the burden on women The State will develop special packages for districts with highest unmet need in terms of health and family welfare services. It will endeavour to increase the utilisation of these services by making them user friendly.

HUMAN DEVELOPMENT INDICATORS

HDI

As of 2011 Chhattisgarh state had a Human Development Index value of 0.537 (medium), ranks 23rd in Indian state. The national average is 0.467 according to 2011 Indian NHDR report.

Standard of living

The Standard of living in Chhattisgarh is extremely imbalanced. The cities such as Raipur, Bhilai and Bilaspur have a medium to high standard of living, while the rural and forested areas lack even the basic resources and amenities. For example-Bhilai has a literacy rate of 86%, while Bastar has a literacy rate of 54% .

Raipur ,The capital of Chhattisgarh is one of the fastest developing cities in India. Atal Nagar (Formerly *Naya Raipur*) is the new planned city that is touted to become the financial hub of the Central Indian region. New world class educational institutions and hospitals have already been established in the city.

Education Index

School children in Chhattisgarh

Chhattisgarh has an Education Index of 0.526 according to the 2011 NHDR, which is higher than that of the states of Bihar, Jharkhand, Uttar Pradesh, Rajasthan. The Average Literacy rate in Chhattisgarh for Urban regions was 84.05 percent in which males were 90.58% literate while female literacy stood at 73.39%. Total literates in urban region of Chhattisgarh were 4,370,966.

According to NSS (2007–08), the literacy rate for Scheduled Tribes (STs) and Scheduled Castes (SCs) was better than the corresponding national average.

Among the marginalised groups, STs are at the bottom of the rankings, further emphasising the lack of social development in the state. Bastar and Dantewada in south Chhattisgarh are the most illiterate districts and the drop out ratio is the highest among all the districts. The reason for this is the extreme poverty in rural areas.

Health Index

As per census 2011, the State has population of 2.55 crore and six medical colleges (five Government and one private) with intake capacity of 700 students and doctor patient ratio of 1:17,000. Under The NITI Aayog released Health Index report titled, "Healthy States, Progressive India."- Chhattisgarh has an index of 52.02 Out of 100, which is better than states such as Madhya Pradesh, Haryana, Rajasthan, Odisha, Bihar , Assam , Uttarakhand and Uttar Pradesh.

Despite different health related schemes and programmes, the health indicators such as percentage of women with BMI<18.5, Under Five Mortality Rate and underweight children are poor. This may be due to the difficulty in accessing the remote areas in the state. The prevalence of female malnutrition in Chhattisgarh is higher than the national average—half of the ST females are malnourished. The performance of SCs is a little better than the corresponding national and state average. The Under Five Mortality Rate among STs is significantly higher than the national average.

Net state domestic product

Chhattisgarh is one of the emerging states with relatively high growth rates of net state domestic product (NSDP) (8.2% vs. 7.1% All India over 2002–2008) and per capita NSDP (6.2% vs. 5.4% All India over 2002–2008). The growth rates of the said parameters are above the national averages and thus it appears that Chhattisgarh is catching up with other states in this respect. However, the state still has very low levels of per capita income as compared to the other states.

Urbanisation

Out of total population of Chhattisgarh, 23.24% people live in urban regions. The total figure of population living in urban areas is 5,937,237 of which 3,035,469 are males and while remaining 2,901,768 are females. Raipur, Durg, Bhilai Nagar, Bilaspur, Korba, Jagdalpur, Rajnandgaon and Raigarh are some of the urban towns and cities in the region.

Sex ratio

There are more than 13 million males and 12.9 million females in Chhattisgarh, which constitutes 2.11% of the country's population. The sex ratio in the state is one of the most balanced in India with 991 females per 1,000 males, as is the child sex-ratio with 964 females per 1,000 males (Census 2011)

Fertility rate

Chhattisgarh has a fairly high fertility rate (3.1) as compared to All India (2.6) and the replacement rate (2.1). It has rural fertility rate of 3.2 and urban fertility rate of 2.1.

SC and ST population

With the exception of the hilly states of the north-east, Chhattisgarh has one of highest shares of Scheduled Tribe (ST) populations within a state, accounting for about 10 percent of the STs in India. Scheduled Castes and STs together constitute more than 50 percent of the state's population. The tribals are an important part of the state population and mainly inhabit the dense forests of Bastar and other districts of south Chhattisgarh. The Scheduled Caste (SC) population of Chhattisgarh is 2,418,722 as per 2001 census constituting 11.6 percent of the total population (20,833,803). The proportion of Scheduled Castes has increased from 11.6 percent in 2001 to 12.8% in 2011. The percentage increase in the population of the scheduled list of tribals during the 2001–2011 decade had been at the rate of 18.23 percent. The share of the tribal population in the entire state had been 30.62 per cent which was 31.76 per cent during 2001.

Poverty

The incidence of poverty in Chhattisgarh is very high. The estimated poverty ratio in 2004–05 based on uniform reference period consumption was around 50 per cent, which is approximately double the all India level. The incidence of poverty in the rural and urban areas is almost the same.

More than half of the rural STs and urban SCs are poor. In general, the proportion of poor SC and ST households in the state is higher than the state average and their community's respective national averages (except for rural SC households). Given that more than 50 per cent of the state's population is ST and SC, the high incidence of income poverty among them is a matter of serious concern in the state.

Tendu Patta (Leaf) collection in Chhattisgarh, India.

This indicates that the good economic performance in recent years has not percolated to this socially deprived group, which is reflected in their poor performance in human development indicators.

Access to drinking water

In terms of access to improved drinking water sources, at the aggregate level, Chhattisgarh fared better than the national average and the SCs of the state performed better than the corresponding national average. Scheduled Tribes are marginally below the state average, but still better than the STs at the all India level.

The proportion of households with access to improved sources of drinking water in 2008–09 was 91%. This proportion was over 90% even in states like Bihar, Chhattisgarh, Madhya Pradesh and Uttar Pradesh. This was largely because these states had over 70% of their households accessing tube wells/ handpumps as sources of drinking water.

Sanitation

Sanitation facilities in the state were abysmally low with only about 41 per cent having toilet facilities before the Swachh Bharat Mission was Launched by the Government of India. The Urban areas of Chhattisgarh attained the title of open defecation free on October 2nd 2017 and the rural areas have achieved a 90.31% sanitation coverage . What sets Chhattisgarh apart from other states of India is an approach to bring in behavioural change in order to get open defecation free status.In Chhattisgarh, people don't get toilet incentives, they have to construct the toilet with their own money, after using the toilet for 3 months they are entitled for the incentive amount.

Teledensity

Across states, it has been found that teledensity (telephone density) was below 10 per cent in 2010 for Chhattisgarh and Jharkhand, reflecting a lack of access to telephones in these relatively poorer states.But due to development of new technology the teledensity in 2017 is 68.08 per cent which shows improvement of telecom infrastructure. On the other hand, for states like Delhi and Himachal Pradesh and metropolitan cities like Kolkata, Mumbai and Chennai, teledensity was over 100 per cent in 2010 implying that individuals have more than one telephone connection.

Road density

The total density of National Highways (NHs) in Chhattisgarh is at 23.4 km per 1,000 km out of the total length of 3,168 km in the State, the Central Government has informed. Chhattisgarh Government had completed construction of 5,266 cement concrete (CC) roads having a total length of 1,530 km in various villages of the State as on May 31, 2016 under 'Mukhyamantri Gram Sadak Yojana'.

2

Culture and Society

CHHATTISGARH

Chhattisgarh, state of east-central India. It is bounded by the Indian states of Uttar Pradeshand Jharkhand to the north and northeast, Odisha (Orissa) to the east, Telangana (formerly part of Andhra Pradesh) to the south, and Maharashtra and Madhya Pradesh to the west. Its capital is Raipur. Area 52,199 square miles (135,194 square km). Pop. (2011) 25,540,196.

Land

Relief

Chhattisgarh is located in the Chhattisgarh Plain, which forms the upper Mahanadi Riverbasin. The basin proper lies at an elevation that ranges from about 800 to 950 feet (250 to 300 metres) above sea level. It is a structural plain with topographic variations resulting from extensive denudation (wearing away of the earth by such processes as weathering and erosion). Knolls, undulating interfluves (areas between adjacent watercourses), and valleys flanked by belts of clayey soils are characteristic of the region. About 100 miles (160 km) wide, the Chhattisgarh Plain is bounded by the Chota Nagpur plateau to the north, the Maikala Range to the west, the hills of Raigarh to the northeast, the Raipur upland to the southeast, and the Bastar plateau to the south. These highlands comprise mostly erosional plateau forms reaching an elevation of more than 2,300 feet (700 metres) in the Maikala Range and the Dandakaranya hills.

Earthquakes are relatively infrequent in Chhattisgarh, though seismic activity of mild intensity has been recorded in northern Chhattisgarh and along the border with Telangana in the south. A few tremors also have been felt in the east and around Raigarh.

Drainage and soils

Chhattisgarh contains the source of one of the most important rivers of the South Asian peninsula—the Mahanadi. This river originates in a village near Raipur. It flows westward for about 125 miles (200 km) and meets the Shivnath River about 8 miles (13 km) from Bilaspur. Thereafter it flows toward the east and enters Odisha, ultimately emptying into the Bay of Bengal. Among the other rivers that drain Chhattisgarh are the Indravati, Arpa, and Pairi.

Various types of soils are found throughout the state. Two types predominate: the black, clayey soils and the red-to-yellow soils. The latter are less fertile and contain substantial amounts of sand.

Climate

The climate in Chhattisgarh is governed by a monsoon weather pattern. The distinct seasons are summer (March to May), winter (November to February), and the intervening rainy months of the southwest monsoon (June to September). The summer is hot, dry, and windy, with high temperatures typically reaching at least 85 °F (about 30 °C) in all parts of the state; in some areas temperatures regularly rise above 100 °F (upper 30s C).

Winters are usually pleasant and dry, with high temperatures in the upper 70s F (mid-20s C). In December and January there is considerable rainfall over the northern part of the state, although the state as a whole receives most of its precipitation during the southwest monsoon. Rainfall usually ranges from 47 to 60 inches (1,200 to 1,500 mm) annually.

Plant and animal life

The eastern and southeastern borderlands of Chhattisgarh are characterized by moist deciduous plantlife, but toward the interior of the state this flora is replaced by dry deciduous vegetation, often degenerating locally into scrub. The most valuable hardwoods are teak and *sal* (*Shorea robusta*). A type of tree called *salai* yields a resin used for incense and medicine, while leaves from *tendu* trees are used for rolling bidi (Indian cigarettes). Bamboo is abundant and is harvested for many purposes.

The forests are home to a broad array of animals, including tigers, striped hyenas, and blackbucks. Other species include the *chital* (spotted deer), gaur (a type of wild buffalo), sambar deer, sloth bear, wild boar, and four-horned antelope, among others. The woodlands are also inhabited by many species of birds. Chhattisgarh has a number of national parks and many wildlife sanctuaries. The Indravati National Park contains a wildlife sanctuary for tigers.

People

Population composition

Chhattisgarh supports a population of diverse ethnic, social, religious, and linguistic backgrounds. More than one-third of the state's residents officially belong to the Scheduled Castes (groups formerly called "untouchables" within the Indian caste system) or to the Scheduled Tribes (indigenous minority peoples who are not embraced by the caste hierarchy). Of the Scheduled Tribes, the Gond peoples are most prominent.

The vast majority of Chhattisgarh's people practice Hinduism, but there are sizable minorities of Muslims, Jains, Christians, and Buddhists. There also is a small community of Sikhs. Hindi, the official language of Chhattisgarh, is the most widely spoken language, followed by Chhattisgarhi. Many of the Gond speak Gondi. Marathi, Urdu, Oriya, Gujarati, and Punjabi are spoken by significant numbers.

Settlement patterns and demographic trends

Some three-fourths of Chhattisgarh's population is rural. The distribution of this population is uneven, however, with the far southern portion of the state having significantly fewer residents than its northern counterpart. The urban population of Chhattisgarh is concentrated mainly in the vicinity of Raipur and Bilaspur in the state's midsection and near Raigarh in the east. However, massive public-sector investment in mining has helped to spur growth around Durg and Bhilai Nagar to the west of Raipur, Korba in the north-central region, and Ambikapur in the northern part of the state. Raipur, Durg–Bhilai Nagar, and Bilaspur have become major urban agglomerations, each with a relatively well-developed industrial base.

Since the late 20th century the rate of population increase in Chhattisgarh has been somewhat below the national average, and men have continued to outnumber women but only slightly. Because it is predominantly agricultural, the state experiences seasonal fluctuations in population. When farming activities come to a virtual halt between January and June, there is mass migration of agricultural workers to Haryana, Punjab, Rajasthan, Delhi, Himachal Pradesh, and anywhere else where there are opportunities for daily wage labour.

Economy

The economy of Chhattisgarh is founded primarily on mining, agriculture, energy production, and manufacturing. The state has major deposits of coal, iron ore, dolomite, and other minerals. The central lowland is known especially for its abundant rice production, and the state as a whole provides the bulk of the country's *tendu* leaves for bidis. Chhattisgarh also is a significant regional supplier of electricity, from both thermal and hydroelectric generators. The state's manufacturing activities focus largely on metals production.

Agriculture

About half of Chhattisgarh's land is farmland, while most of the remainder is either under forest cover or is otherwise unsuitable for cultivation. Roughly three-fourths of the farmland is under cultivation.

Often called the country's rice bowl, the central lowland plain supplies grain to hundreds of rice mills. Maize and millet dominate the highlands. Cotton and oilseeds are the important commercial crops of the region. Agriculture continues to be characterized in many areas by the use of manual methods of cultivation; farmers in the basin have been particularly slow to adopt mechanized agricultural techniques.

Livestock and poultry farming also are prominent. The state's livestock includes cows, buffalo, goats, sheep, and pigs. There are several centres for improving the quality of these animals, such as those for the artificial insemination and crossbreeding of goats in Bilaspur and Dhar.

Resources and power

Chhattisgarh is mineral-rich. Although many of the state's resources remain to be exploited fully, its major reserves of coal, iron ore, limestone, bauxite, and dolomite, as well as its significant deposits of tin, manganese ore, gold, and copper, make the mining industry a major source of income. In fact, Chhattisgarh is one of the country's largest suppliers of dolomite. Its iron ore, which is of top quality, is found primarily in the south-central and southern parts of the state. Deposits of diamonds have been discovered near Raipur.

Chhattisgarh produces more power than it consumes. The bulk of the state's power comes from thermal power plants, several of which are near Korba. However, the state also is well endowed with potential sources of hydroelectric energy. Main hydroelectric projects (jointly developed with other states) are the Ban Sagar dam, with Bihar and Uttar Pradesh, and the Harked dam over the Mahanadi River. The Hasdeo Bango hydroelectric power project is near Korba.

Manufacturing

Chhattisgarh has been industrializing—slowly but certainly—since the late 20th century. As part of this planned development, the government has established a number of industrial estates, notably at Raipur and Bhilai Nagar.

There now are dozens of large- and medium-scale steel industries producing hot metal, pig iron, sponge iron, rails, ingots, and plates; Bhilai Nagar is the site of an especially large iron-and-steel plant. Many of the metal industries, as well as other emergent enterprises such as the production of microelectronics and high-tech optical fibres, receive government support.

In the private sector there are cement works, as well as assorted mills producing paper, sugar, textiles (cotton, wool, silk, and jute), lumber, flour, and oil (from oilseeds). A number of factories manufacture fertilizer, synthetic fibres, and chemicals. Most small-scale industries of Chhattisgarh are centred on the production of traditional handiworks, including textiles (such as saris), carpets, pottery, and gold- and silver-thread embroidery.

Transportation

Chhattisgarh is well connected to the rest of the country by road, rail, and air. The state is traversed by two of the national highways, as well as by some of the major rail routes. Most of Chhattisgarh's larger cities are the sites of important railway junctions. There are airports at Raipur and Bilaspur.

Government And Society

The structure of Chhattisgarh's government, like that of most other Indian states, is defined by the national constitution of 1950. The head of state—the governor—is appointed by the president of India. The governor is aided and advised by a chief minister, who heads the Council of Ministers, which is responsible to the elected Legislative Assembly (Vidhan Sabha). Although the political capital of Chhattisgarh is Raipur, the High Court is located in Bilaspur. A chief justice presides over the High Court.

Local government includes several divisions, which are subdivided further into districts. Each division is administered by a commissioner, while each is headed by a collector. Collectors exercise both executive and magisterial power.

A large area of Chhattisgarh is under the control of the Naxalites (Maoist guerrillas). Indeed, in several pockets of Bastar division in the south, state law has at times failed to function. The conflict ultimately has hampered the development of this fertile area.

History

The history of the Chhattisgarh region dates back to about the 4th century CE, when it was known as Southern (or South) Kosala. The name Chhattisgarh, meaning "thirty-six forts," was formerly applied to the territory of the Haihaya dynasty of Ratanpur, founded about 750. Under British rule the present region of Chhattisgarh consisted of a division comprising 14 feudatory princely kingdoms under the Eastern States Agency. Raipur was the headquarters of that division.

Within the Republic of India, Chhattisgarh was part of Madhya Pradesh until Nov. 1, 2000. Although the campaign for Chhattisgarh statehood began in earnest only in the 1970s, its roots go back to the early 20th century, when local leaders began to claim a distinct cultural identity for the region. In the early 1990s the push for statehood was manifested in the election platforms of various political parties, and promises of a separate state were again prominent during the elections of 1996 and 1998. In August 2000 the Indian legislature passed the Madhya Pradesh Reorganization Bill to create Chhattisgarh. The formation of Chhattisgarh was especially noteworthy in that it was peaceful; it was not associated with any of the agitation and violence that marred the establishment of two other new states—Uttaranchal (now Uttarakhand) and Jharkhand—about the same time.

CULTURE

The state hosts many religious sects such as Satnami Panth, Kabirpanth, Ramnami Samaj and others. Champaran (Chhattisgarh) is a small town with religious significance as the birthplace of the Saint Vallabhacharya, increasingly important as a pilgrimage site for the Gujarati community.

Chhattisgarh has a significant role in the life of lord Rama. Lord Rama along with his wife Sita and his younger brother Lakshaman had started his Vanvas (exile) in the Bastar region (more precisely Dandakaranya region) of Chhattisgarh. They lived more than 10 of their 14 years of Vanvas in different places of Chhattisgarh. One of the remarkable place is Shivrinarayan which is nearby Bilaspur district of Chhattisgarh. Shivrinarayan was named after an old lady Shabari. When Ram visited Shabari she said "I do not have anything to offer other than my heart, but here are some berry fruits. May it please you, my Lord." Saying so, Shabari offered the fruits she had meticulously collected to Rama. When Rama was tasting them, Lakshmana raised the concern that Shabari had already tasted them and therefore unworthy of eating. To this Rama said that of the many types of food he had tasted, "nothing could equal these berry fruits, offered with such devotion. You taste them, then alone will you know. Whomsoever offers a fruit, leaf, flower or some water with love, I partake it with great joy."

A carving in the 10th- or 11th-century Hindu temple of Malhar village. This area, 40 km from Bilaspur, was supposedly a major Buddhist centre in ancient times.

The Odia culture is prominent in the eastern parts of Chhattisgarh bordering Odisha.

Literature

Chhattisgarh is a storehouse of literature, performing arts and crafts—all of which derives its substance and sustenance from the day-to-day life experiences of its people. Religion, mythology, social and political events, nature and folklore are favourite motifs. Traditional crafts include painting, woodcarving, bell metal craft, bamboo ware and tribal jewellery. Chhattisgarh has a rich literary heritage with roots that lie deep in the sociological and historical movements of the region. Its literature reflects the regional consciousness and the evolution of an identity distinct from others in Central India.

Crafts

Chhattisgarh is known for "Kosa silk" and "lost wax art". Besides saris and salwar suits, the fabric is used to create lehengas, stoles, shawls and menswear including jackets, shirts, achkans and sherwanis. Works by the internationally renowned sculptor, Sushil Sakhuja's Dhokra Nandi, are available at government's Shabagcrafts emporium, Raipur.

Dance

Panthi, Rawat Nacha, Pandwani, Chaitra, Kaksar, Saila, Khamb-swang, Bhatra Naat, Rahas, Raai, Maao-Pata and Soowa are the several indigenous dance styles of Chhattisgarh.

Panthi

, the folk dance of the Satnami community, has religious overtones. Panthi is performed on Maghi Purnima, tbla the anniversary of the birth of Guru Ghasidas. The dancers dance around a jaitkhamb set up for the occasion, to songs eulogising their spiritual head. The songs reflect a view of *nirvana*, conveying the spirit of their guru's renunciation and the teachings of saint poets like Kabir, Ramdas and Dadu. Dancers with bent torsos and swinging arms dance, carried away by their devotion. As the rhythm quickens, they perform acrobatics and form human pyramids.

Pandwani

Pandavani is a folk ballad form performed predominantly in Chhattisgarh. It depicts the story of the Pandavas, the leading characters in the epic Mahabharata. The artists in the Pandavani narration consist of a lead artist and some supporting singers and musicians. There are two styles of narration in Pandavani, Vedamati and Kapalik. In the Vedamati style the lead artist narrates in a simple manner by sitting on the floor throughout the performance. The Kaplik style is livelier, where the narrator actually enacts the scenes and characters.

Pandwani

Raut Nacha

Raut Nacha

Raut Nacha, the folk dance of cowherds, is a traditional dance of Yaduvanshis (clan of Yadu) as symbol of worship to Krishna from the 4th day of Diwali (Goverdhan Puja) till the time of Dev Uthani Ekadashi (day of awakening of the gods after a brief rest) which is the 11th day after Diwali according to the Hindu calendar. The dance closely resembles Krishna's dance with the gopis (milkmaids). In Bilaspur, the Raut Nach Mahotsav folk dance festival is organised annually since 1978. Tens of hundreds of Rautt dancers from remote areas participate.

Soowa Nacha

Soowa or Suwa tribal dance in Chhattisgarh is also known as Parrot Dance. It is a symbolic form of dancing related to worship. Dancers keep a parrot in a bamboo-pot and form a circle around it. Then performers sing and dance, moving around it with clapping. This is one of the main dance form of tribal women of Chhattisgarh.

Sua Nacha at Khudmudi Village, Chhattisgarh

Karma

Tribal groups like Gonds, the Baigas and the Oraons in Chhattisgarh have Karma dance as part of their culture. Both men and women arrange themselves in two rows and follow the rhythmic steps, directed by the singer group. The Karma tribal dance marks the end of the rainy season and the advent of spring season.

CUISINE OF CHHATTISGARH

Most of the traditional and tribal foods are made of rice and rice flour, curd and a variety of green leafy vegetables like lal bhaaji, chowlai bhaaji, chech bhaji, kaanda bhaaji, kheksi,kathal,kochai patta, kohda and bohar bhaji. Badi and

Bijori are optional food categories; gulgula (bobra), bidiya, dhoodh fara, bafauli, kusli, balooshahi,singhara, tikhur ,anarsa and khurmi fall in sweet categories. Some well known breakfast dishes made out of Rice & rice flour include fara/muthiya (rice rolls in white sauce), cheela(dosa like dish made with rice batter), angakar roti, chousela roti (rice puris), etc. One of the common meal had during the scorching summer is Bore Baasi (literally means dipped rice from last cooked meal) which mainly consists of cooked rice dipped water/dahi/buttermilk. It is mostly accompanied by pickle and raw onion. It helps maintain the water levels in the body, keeping it cool and hydrated during the hot and arid summer days.

One of the well known traditional dishes of Chhattisgarh is Iddhar. It is made with ground Urad dal and kochai patta. Both are arranged in alternate layers 2-3 time and then rolled. This roll is then cooked in steam and cut into pieces. After that it is prepared with curd like curry. Some people also make it with gram flour (besan) instead of urad dal. Tribal and village populations drink a brew made of the small, creamy white flower of a local tree called Mahuwa.

CULTURAL HERITAGE

Chhattisgarh, a little paradise in central India, is not only known for its exceptional scenic beauty, but the region also has a history of its own. Famous for its unique and varied tribal populations, including the world-famous Gonds tribes of Bastar region, Chhattisgarh has a rich cultural heritage, dating back to thousands of years. Chhattisgarh has its own unique form of dances, music, religious beliefs (each tribe has their own gods), cuisine, tribal festivals and more, offering a cultural destination with a difference. The Dusshera Festival at Bastar is famous in all over India and celebrated by tribes with great fanfare.

Chhattisgarh is also known for its rich and unique architectural monuments including temples, caves, palaces, providing insights into the rich cultural heritage of the region. There are number of important heritage sites, which you can visit on your cultural tour of Chhattisgarh. Bhoramdeo, Dantewada, Deepadih, Dongargarh, Jogibhatta, Rajim, Sirpur, Malhar, Sita Bhengra, and Sheorinarayan are the major sites for heritage tourism in Chhattisgarh. The rock-paintings of Singhanpur, Sita Bhengra, and Kabra mountains are worth visiting on your cultural tour of Chhattisgarh.

Chhattisgarh is also rich in arts and crafts. The tribes of Bastar were amongst the earliest to work with metal in India. The wooden figurines of gods, animals, oil lamps, carts and bamboo furniture, clay pieces made by tribes are very famous and worth purchasing souvenirs.

FESTIVALS

Chhattisgarh is one of the most fascinating and colourful states of India. Known for its exceptional scenic beauty and the unique tribal populations, Chhattisgarh has a number of vivid and colourful festivals, held all round the year. The famous and widely celebrated festivals of Chhattisgarh include the Dusshera, Deepavali, Holi, Govardhan Pooja, Pola, Nawakhai and many others are celebrated with great vividness and festivity.

Dusshera is the most famous festivals of Chhattisgarh and is celebrated with great fanfare in Bastar region. During this occasion, all the deities from all the tribal villages congregate at the Temple of goddess Danteshwari in Jagdalpur, the district headquarters of Bastar. Dusshera in Bastar is quite different from the Dusshera of North India and has nothing to do with the triumphant return of lord Rama in Ayodhya. Bastar Dusshera is devoted entirely to goddess Danteshwari and celebrated with great gaiety by all major tribes of Bastar. Madai Festival is another famous festival of Bastar region held in the different villages extending from Mandla to Bastar. It's quite popular among Gond tribes of Bastar and thousands of devotees gather under the shade of a sacred tree to sacrifice a goat to the mother goddess and the whole night is spent in dancing, eating and making merry.

Bhagoriya Festival is a popular festival among Bhil tribes of the region and Bhagoradev or the god of dance is worshipped on this occasion. During this festival young girls and boys dance with each other and express their love to opposite sex. Kajari Festival is another important festival of Chhattisgarh region, which falls on the same day as Raksha Bandhan that is on the Shravan Purnima. In addition there are many festivals in Chhattisgarh, which are related to agriculture. Hariyali, Kora, Navakhani and Cherta Festivals are the most important agricultural festivals of Chhattisgarh.

Chhattisgarh also organizes many colourful fairs in different towns and cities of the state, all round the year. Rajim Lochan Mahotsav held every year from 16th February till 1st March is celebrated with great fanfare. Bhoramdeo Mahotsav (last week of March), Chakradhar Festival (September or October), Goncha Festival (July), Narayanpur Mela (last week of February) and Sheorinarayan Fair (February) are other widely celebrated and most enjoyed fairs and festivals of Chhattisgarh.

EMERGING IDENTITY AND SOCIO-CULTURAL SPACES

The socio-religious reform movements and the tribal rebellions, contributed, although indirectly to emerging consciousness in the region. Guru Ghasidas clearly articulated the need to consolidate and create regional consciousness and solidarity to fight against exploitation. Similarly, other sects with their message of equality and solidarity also influenced the unfolding regional narrative.

The tribal rebellions deeply affected the political, social and economic discourse of Chhattisgarh. The issue of people's rights over local resources was brought centre stage. It also raised the fundamental question of identity and preserving traditional culture and way of life. The evolution and formation of a formal Chhattisgarh identity coincided with the national movement and it was in this period that the process of crystallisation of a Chhattisgarh identity was initiated and a distinct identity started emerging and taking definite shape in the social and cultural sphere.

Pandit Sunderlal Sharma, Thakur Pyarelal Singh and Khub Chand Baghel were members of the Indian National Congress and some of the prominent leaders of the national movement in Chhattisgarh.

These leader did not confine themselves merely to political activity; they were involved in initiating as well as actively participating in socio-cultural reform movements. These leaders also reiterated the fact that Chhattisgarh had a distinct socio-cultural identity and used this as a base for reform encourage the formation of a Chhattisgarhi consciousness amongst the masses through literacy drives cultural activities and social reform programmes.

The literature of the period also reflected the search for and an attempt to establish a distinctive identity. As early as 1901, M R Sapre from Pendra Road published a magazine called' Chhattisgarh Mitra' which focused on the region.

Khub Chand Baghel who was waging a struggle against untouchability wrote plays called 'Jarnail Singh' and 'Unch Neech'. During this period, leaders were also writing plays that focused on social issues in the context of Chhattisgarhi identity. Pt. Sundarlal Sharma wrote 'Daan Lila' and R.C. Deshmukh wrote 'Naacha' and 'Gumbad'. Vaman Rao Deshmukh, an important cooperative leader of the times was specifically writing about the identity of Chhattisgarh.

Pandit Sundar Lala Sharma who was one of the most prominent leaders of Central India, fought against the caste system and worked continuously for an improvement in the condition of dalits. In 1917, he broke the forest laws in Sihawa with the support of the tribals. Three years later, in 1920, Pt. Sharma initiated the Nahar Satyagrah in Kandal village, Durg district, against the tax on water.

In 1925, he entered a temple with a group of dalits. Thakur Pyarelal Singh, also known as the father of the cooperative movement in Chhattisgarh, was a Gandhian with a reformatory zeal. He organised the first labour movement of Chhattisgarh in Rajnandgaon in 1920. This movement was started to demand a fixed number of working hours. Later in the same region, the second and the third labour movement of 1924 and 1925 were also organised under the leadership of Pyare Lal Singh.

By the time India gained Independence in 1947, the discourse on regional identity had changed its focus from social reform movements to the issue of exploitation of Chhattisgarh. Multiple channels of expression of this demand were used.

A journal called ' Chhattisgarh Chhatisgarhion Ka or Chhattisgarh belongs to the people of Chhattisgarh was started by Khub Chand Baghel. Another journal called ' Chhattisgarh Atma Ki Pukar' or The voice of the Soul of Chhattisgarh which also dealt with the same issues was also published and is especially looked into the significance of possessing a cultural identity and initiated a movement for establishing pride in Chhattisgarhi culture.

In 1956, Chedi Lal Barrister with the support of Khub Chand Baghel organised the Chhattisgarh Mahasabha at Rajnandgaon.

This meeting was attended by members of all parties and was supported by various caste groups and associations of Chhattisgarh. It is reported that the Mahasabha was attended by more than 50,000 people.

The Mahasabha passed a resolution stating that the 'Art and Culture of Chhattisgarh should get fair opportunity to grow'. A decision to launch the journal ' Chhattisgarh' was taken. The Mahasabha unanimously resolved to work towards solving the problems of the region as well as to struggle for the rights of Chhattisgarh.

The movement for consolidating the Chhattisgarh identity has continued through the decades. It would become dormant for some years and then against erupt in some other district. It is therefore, impossible to create a linear pattern of the creation of Chhattisgarh identity. However, it is important to underscore that the multilayered and multilateral process of formulating and expressing Chhattisgarhi identity took place over a long period of time. Various other political and non-political formations have, within the framework of their ideological positions and worldview, been working towards the formation of an identity for Chhattisgarh.

Chhattisgarh Samaj an organisation formed under the umbrella of the Proutist Sarva Samaj Samiti has working for the development of a political, social and cultural consciousness of Chhattisgarh.

Since the late sixties the Samaj has been publishing a weekly news paper in Chhattisgarhi through which they have been working for the growth of the Chhattisgarhi language.

Through the different wings of the Samja, an attempt is being made to spread regional consciousness which they believe will then translate into the development of Chhattisgarh. A diametrically opposite non-party political formation struggling for the identity of Chhattisgarh is Chhattisgarh Mukti Morcha or the CMM.

This mass based peoples movement started as a trade union movement and then moved on to link the exploitation of the region to the fact that its cultural identity had been suppressed. Gradually the movement started focusing on the struggle of Chhattisgarh against the exploitative oppressive and hegemonic mainstream. On 19 December, 1979, in an attempt to link the tradition of struggle to the ethos of Chhattisgarh, the CMM then the CMSS, initiated the tradition of observing Shahid Vir Narain Singh's date of execution by the British as martyr's day.

The identity of Chhattisgarh has been created and evolved through a complex process that has largely charted its own course. A combination of cultural historical social economic and political factors have contributed to this process. The wide pluralities of cultures, traditions, histories and customs existing in the region have combined to form a unique mixture that has fed into the development of the Chhattisgarh ethos and identity. However, the key point is that the identity of Chhattisgarh cannot be viewed as separate form the people of Chhattisgarh. It is important to note that the Chhattisgarh identity has been asserted in different forms and has become more pronounced in adverse circumstances manifesting itself especially as protest against exploitation.

Dr. H L Shukla distinguishes between self image and other image for a more holistic understanding of Chhattisgarh identity and ethos. It is imperative to synthesize and blend the two images to understand the priorities and challenges facing new Chhattisgarh. The identity of Chhattisgarh is an inclusive identity, in spite of the movement for Prathak Chhattisgarh. There exists in the Chhattisgarh identity while being sensitive towards as well as protecting and preserving the plurality of customs, traditions and cultures.

3

Government and Politics

GOVERNMENT OF CHHATTISGARH

The Structure of a State Government is as follows

The state has three types of functions:

(i) Legislative

(ii) Judicial

(iii) Executive

Since Independence, there has been a tremendous growth in the executive functions of the state, due to:

(i) Growth in the traditional functions of the state like law and order, education, public health, etc.

(ii) New functions, such as promoting economic development and social and economic justice undertaken by the state.

This has consequently led to a large expansion in the executive machinery of the state.

In the state level, there are Cabinet Ministers and Ministers of State

GOVERNANCE AND ADMINISTRATION

The State Legislative assembly is composed of 90 members of the Legislative Assembly. There are 11 members of the Lok

Sabha from Chhattisgarh. The Rajya Sabha has five members from the state.

Districts

Chhattisgarh comprises 27 districts. The following are the list of the districts of Chhattisgarh State:

1. Balod
2. Baloda Bazar-Bhatapara
3. Balrampur
4. Bastar
5. Bemetara
6. Bijapur
7. Bilaspur
8. Dantewada
9. Dhamtari
10. Durg
11. Gariaband
12. Janjgir-Champa
13. Jashpur
14. Kanker
15. Kabirdham
16. Kondagaon
17. Korba
18. Koriya
19. Mahasamund
20. Mungeli
21. Narayanpur
22. Raigarh
23. Raipur
24. Rajnandgaon
25. Surguja
26. Sukma
27. Surajpur.

CHHATTISGARH DIVISION

Chhattisgarh Division was a former administrative division of the Central Provinces of British India. It was located in the east of the Central Provinces and encompassed the upper Mahanadi River basin, in the central part of present-day Chhattisgarh state of India.

With the advent of the British the town of Raipur, headquarters of Chhattisgarh Division, gained prominence over Ratanpur, the historical capital of the territory. The Central Provinces became the Central Provinces and Berar in 1936 until the Independence of India.

History

Chhattisgarh Division was occupied by the Bhonsle Marathas and incorporated into the Kingdom of Nagpur in the 18th century. The Kingdom of Nagpur was annexed to British India in 1853, becoming Nagpur Province. In 1861 Nagpur Province was merged with the Saugor and Nerbudda Territories to form the Central Provinces. All the princely states of the Central Provinces were in Chhattisgarh Division, except for Makrai, which was in the Hoshangabad District of the Nerbudda Division.

In 1905, most of Sambalpur District and the princely states of Bamra, Rairakhol, Sonpur, Patna, and Kalahandi were transferred to Bengal Province and the princely states of Changbhakar, Korea, Surguja, Udaipur, and Jashpur were transferred from Bengal to the Central Provinces.

In 1933 the princely states in Chhattisgarh Division were transferred to the Eastern States Agency. On 24 October 1936, the Central Provinces became the Central Provinces and Berar when they were fully merged with Berar Province, although Berar remained under the nominal sovereignty of Hyderabad State.

Territory

The Chhattisgarh Division was bounded to the north by the

Chota Nagpur States, to the east by the Orissa Tributary States, to the south by the princely states of Bastar and Kanker, and on the west by Nagpur and Jabalpur divisions, as well as the princely statesof Kawardha, Khairagarh, and Nandgaon.

Districts

The division included the following three districts:

- Raipur
- Bilaspur
- Sambalpur

GOVERNMENT OF CHHATTISGARH

The Government of Chhattisgarh also known as the State Government of Chhattisgarh, or locally as State Government, is the supreme governing authority of the Indian state of Chhattisgarh and its 27 districts. It consists of an executive, led by the Governor of Chhattisgarh, a judiciary and a legislative branch.

Like other states in India, the head of state of Chhattisgarh is the Governor, appointed by the President of India on the advice of the Central government. His or her post is largely ceremonial. The Chief Minister is the head of government and is vested with most of the executive powers. Raipur is the capital of Chhattisgarh, and houses the Chhattisgarh Vidhan Sabha (Legislative Assembly) and the secretariat. The Chhattisgarh High Court, located Bilaspur, has jurisdiction over the whole state.

The present Legislative Assembly of Chhattisgarh is unicameral, consisting of 91 Members of Legislative Assembly (M.L.A) (90 elected and one nominated). Its term is 5 years, unless sooner dissolved.

- Founder Chief Minister of Chhattisgarh State "Mr. Ajeet Pramod Kumar Jogi" From Congress Party
- Second Chief Minister of Chhattisgarh State "Dr. Raman Singh" From Bhartiya Janta Party

CHHATTISGARH LEGISLATIVE ASSEMBLY

The Chhattisgarh Vidhan Sabha or the Chhattisgarh Legislative Assembly is the unicameral state legislature of Chhattisgarhstate in central India. The seat of the Vidhan Sabha is at Raipur, the capital of the state. The Vidhan Sabha comprises 91 Members of Legislative Assembly, which include 90 members directly elected from single-seat constituencies and 1 nominated from the Anglo-Indian community. Its term is 5 years, unless sooner dissolved.

History

The state of Chhattisgarh was created by the Madhya Pradesh Reorganization Act 2000, approved by the President of India on 25 August 2000. The Chhattisgarh Vidhan Sabha came into existence with the creation of the state on 1 November 2000. The first session of the Chhattisgarh Vidhan Sabha was held at Jashpur hall of Rajkumar College in Raipur. Later, the Vidhan Sabha was shifted to the newly constructed Chhattisgarh Vidhan Sabha Bhavan at Vidhan Nagar, on Raipur-Baloda Bazar Road.

LIST OF CHIEF MINISTERS OF CHHATTISGARH

The Chief Minister of Chhattisgarh is the chief executive of the central Indian state of Chhattisgarh. As per the Constitution of India, the Governor of Chhattisgarh is a state's *de jure* head, but *de facto* executive authority rests with the chief minister. Following elections to the Chhattisgarh Legislative Assembly, the state's governor usually invites the party (or coalition) with a majority of seats to form the government. The governor appoints the chief minister, whose council of ministers are collectively responsible to the assembly. Given that he has the confidence of the assembly, the chief minister's term is for five years and is subject to no term limits.

Since Chhattisgarh was created in 2000, when it was carved out of the tribal-dominated southern districts of Madhya Pradesh, two people have served as the state's chief minister. The first was the Indian National Congress party's Ajit Jogi, who served for three years from 2000 to 2003. After Jogi's departure, since 7 December 2003, Raman Singh of the Bharatiya Janata Party has been the incumbentChief Minister of Chhattisgarh.

LIST OF GOVERNORS OF CHHATTISGARH

The Governor of Chhattisgarh is a nominal head and representative of the President of India in the state of Chhattisgarh. The Governor is appointed by the President for a maximum period of 5 years. The current governor, since 15th August 2018 is Anandiben Patel.

Powers and functions

The Governor enjoys many different types of powers:

- Executive powers related to administration, appointments and removals,
- Legislative powers related to lawmaking and the state legislature, that is Vidhan Sabha or Vidhan Parishad, and
- Discretionary powers to be carried out according to the discretion of the Governor.

Governors of Chhattisgarh

#	Name	Took Office	Left Office
1	D. N. Sahay	1 November 2000	1 June 2003
2	Krishna Mohan Seth	2 June 2003	25 January 2007
3	E. S. L. Narasimhan	25 January 2007	23 January 2010
4	Shekhar Dutt	23 January 2010	19 June 2014
—	Ram Naresh Yadav (Acting)	19 June 2014	14 July 2014
5	Balram Das Tandon	18 July 2014	14 August 2018
—	Anandiben Patel (Acting)	15 August 2018	till date

CHHATTISGARH HIGH COURT

The Chhattisgarh High Court is one of the High Courts in India located at village Bodri, Bilaspur with jurisdiction over the state of Chhattisgarh. It was established on 1 November 2000 with the creation of new state of Chhattisgarh upon the reorganisation of the state of Madhya Pradesh. The High Court of Bilaspur is the 19th High Court of India

Justice R. S. Garg was the first acting Chief Justice of the Chhattisgarh High Court. The court has a sanctioned judge strength of eighteen.

Judges of the High Court

- Hon'ble The Chief Justice
- Justice Pritinker Diwaker
- Justice Prashant Mishra
- Justice Manindra Mohan Shrivastava
- Justice Goutam Bhaduri
- Justice Sanjay K. Agrawal
- Justice P. Sam Koshy
- Justice Rajendra Chandra Singh Samant
- Justice Sharad Kumar Gupta
- Justice Ram Prasanna Sharma
- Justice Arvind Sigh Chandel
- Justice Parth Prateem Sahu
- Justice Gautam Chouridya
- Justice Vimla Singh Kapoor
- Justice Rajani Dubey

Former Chief Justices

- Justice R.S. Garg, joined as Acting Chief Justice on 1 November 2000 and officiated till 4 December 2000
- Justice W.A. Shishak, joined as the Chief Justice on 4 December 2000 and officiated till 6 February 2002
- Justice K.H.N. Kuranga, joined as the Chief Justice on 6 February 2002 and officiated till 28 May 2004
- Justice A.S.V. Moorthy, joined as the Chief Justice on 28 May 2004 and officiated till 14 March 2005

- Justice A.K. Patnaik, joined as the Chief Justice on 14 March 2005 and officiated till 2 February 2008
- Justice S.R. Nayak
- Justice H.L. Dattu
- Justice Rajeev Gupta, joined as the Chief Justice on 2 February 2008 and officiated till 10 October 2012
- Justice Yatindra Singh
- Justice Navin Sinha
- Justice Deepak Gupta
- Justice A M Sapre, joined as Acting Chief Justice on 10 October2012 and officiated till 23 October 2012
- Justice T.B. Radhakrishnan

Former Judges of the High Court who are serving Judges of the Supreme Court of India

- Justice H.L. Dattu, Former Chief Justice of India,
- Justice A.K. Patnaik.
- Justice Abhay Manohar Sapre, present Judge, Supreme Court of India.
- Justice Navin Sinha
- Justice Deepak Gupta

Chhattisgarh High Court Bar Association

Chhattisgarh High Court Bar Association is the representative body of advocates practicing in Bilaspur High Court elected by way of direct voting from about 2400 members of the Bar Association and its officials have a term of two years.

POLICY IMPLEMENTATION MECHANISM

An operational plan will be prepared for each policy intervention with details of specific activities to be implemented. Roles and responsibilities of people/department and time frame with outcomes will be developed. At the state level the State Health Mission will be constituted with the Chief Minister as Chairperson, the Health and Family Welfare Secretary as

Member Secretary and representatives of other development departments and other sectors such as NGOs, organisation and professional bodies as members. The District Health Society will be entrusted with the responsibility of planning for monitoring and the implementation of the Chhattisgarh State Integrated Health and Population Policy at the district level.

Conclusion: The State is judged by the well being of its people, as reflected in levels of health, nutrition and education; by the civil and political liberties enjoyed by their citizens; by the protection guaranteed to children and by provisions made for the vulnerable and the disadvantaged.

The people of Chhattisgarh can be its greatest asset if they are provided with the means to lead a healthy and economically productive life. Comprehensive primary health care and population stabilisation is a multi-sector endeavour requiring effective dialogue and coordination at all levels of the government and the society. Spread of literacy and education, increasing availability of primary health care services, convergence of service delivery at village level, participation of women together with a steady, equitable involvement in family resources will facilitate early achievement of socio-demographic goals.

In the area of public health an improved standard of governance is a prerequisite for the success of any health and population policy. The success of the Integrated Health and Population Policy in consonance with the National Population Policy 2000 and the National Health Policy 2002 will fulfil the aspirations of the people of Chhattisgarh.

POWER OF THE STATE GOVERNMENT

Not withstanding anything contained in the forgoing paragraphs of the Integrated Health and Population Policy, the State Government by issuance of notification in the official gazette may amend or withdraw any of the provisions and/or the schemes mentioned herein. If any difficulty arises in giving effect to provisions of the Integrated Health and Population Policy and/or any dispute arises about the interpretation of any provisions of the said policy, the same shall be referred to the Chief Minister through Chief Secretary and thereon the decision taken shall be final.

Overview: The state of Chhattisgarh is spread over an area of 135194 square kilometers and comprises of sixteen districts of Koriya, Surguja and Jashpurnagar to the north, Korba, Bilaspur, Janjgir Chhampa and Raigarh in the North central, Kawardah, Rajnandgaon, Durg, Raipur, Dhamtari and Mahasamnd in the centre and Kanker, Bastar and Dantewara in the South. According to the 1991 Census, the total population residing in the Chhattisgarh was 1.761 crores, which was 2.1 percent of the population of India. The state of Chhattisgarh is carved out of 30.49 percent of the land area and 26.6 percent of the population of the undivided Madhya Pradesh.

The state of Chhattisgarh has 20378 village of which 19,720 are inhabited villages. The state have a total of 96 tehsils and 146 janpad panchayats or blocks. Out of the total 465 cities and towns of the undivided Madhya Pradesh, 95 cities & towns is in Chhattisgarh, including 6 Class 12 towns.

Gender: The gender ratio for Chhattisgarh according to the 1991 census was 985, which is very high when compared to most other regions of India. Except for Kerala, the new state of Chhattisgarh has a higher gender ratio than all other states. This does not include a comparison with the two other new states of Uttaranchal and Vananchal.

The gender ratio in Rural areas is 1000, but the urban gender ratio, on the other hand is very low at just 917. The trend of a very low urban gender ratio is common across different groups in Chhattisgarh. The gender ratio amongst the tribal groups in the state, based on the 1991 census was 1009, but it falls to a low of just 920 for urban areas. Similarly the gender ratio for all scheduled castes was 987, whereas it was 853 in urban areas. It is not only the tribal communities that have a high gender ratio. The non-scheduled tribes and castes have a gender ratio of 971 in 1991. This figure is high and shows that women in Chhattisgarh are in a better condition in comparison to most of India.

Out of the sixteen districts that comprise Chhattisgarh, eight had a gender ratio of over 1000 in 1991. It has generally been seen that Scheduled Tribes have a gender ratio of over a 1000, but in the Chhattisgarh districts that have a relatively lower Scheduled Tribes population, the gender ratios have been higher. Janjgir Chhampa has a gender ratio of 1007, but only 12.2 percent tribals Kawardha has a gender ratio of 996 and a Scheduled Tribe population of 20 percent, Raipur has a gender ratio of 983 while its Scheduled Tribe population is 13 percent. Dhamtari's gender ratio is 1009 and its Scheduled Tribe population is 27 percent and Mahasamund has a gender ratio of 1015 and a Scheduled Tribe population of 28 percent.

The Infant Mortality Rate for the girl child in Chhattisgarh was 83 per 1000 live births in 1991. Looking at the over all trends in the IMR of undivided Madhya Pradesh, it has dropped from 119 for females in 1991 to 90 in 1997, and we can expect that the female IMR in Chhattisgarh would also have declined by around ten to fifteen percent. The female life expectancy at birth in 1991, according to estimates derived from Census data was 62 years.

The Worker Participation Rate of 41 percent for women in Chhattisgarh is much higher than the Worker Participation Rate of 29.6 percent for Madhya Pradesh. About 92 percent of main workers amongst women were engaged in agriculture in 1991.

CHHATTISGARH MUKTI MORCHA

Chhattisgarh Mukti Morcha (Chhattisgarh Liberation Front), political party in the Indian state of Chhattisgarh.

On the 3rd of March 1977 the Chhattisgarh Mines Shramik Sangh (Chhattisgarh Mines Workers Union) was founded by Shankar Guha Niyogi. 1982 CMSS formed CMM as their political front. CMM was formed to fight for the cultural identity of the region and for upliftment for the workers and peasants. CMM organized social campaigns, such as against alcohol abuse and instituted social projects, such as workers' financied hospital. Niyogi was murdered in Bhilai 1991.

Today Janak Lal Thakur is the president of CMM and Anoop Singh its secretary.

The motto of CMMs is Sangharsh aur Nirman (Struggle and Construction). Another motto is Virodh Nahi Vikalp (Not resistance, but alternative).

CMM was neutral on the issue of formation of a separate Chhattisgarh state. CMM is very active in the struggle against genetically modified seeds.

In the legislative assembly elections in Chhattisgarh 2003 CMM had put up eight candidates, whom together mustered 37 335 votes.

CHHATTISGARH VIKAS PARTY

Chhattisgarh Vikas Party, an extremely short-lived political party in Chhattisgarh, India. CVP was formed on December 20, 2002 when 12 members of the state legislative assembly belonging to the Bharatiya Janata Party broke away. CVP was led by Tarun Chatterji. CVP was recognized by the Congress-affiliated Speaker of the assembly. The following day CVP merged into the Indian National Congress.

RASHTRIYA JANTANTRIK DAL

Rashtriya Jantantrik Dal (National Democratic Party), a political party in India, former when former Union minister and NCP Chhattisgarh state president Vidhya Charan Shukla broke away from the Nationalist Congress Party on February 5, 2004. Shukla was the party president. RJD merged with Bharatiya Janata Party on March 13, 2004.

PUCL State Convention Aims at Defending Democracy with all its Might: The Chhattisgarh branch of People's Union for Civil Liberties (PUCL) has been duly constituted at the General Body Meeting on 28th March at Raipur. Two national observers conducted the proceedings, where a 19-member State Council and 13-member Executive Committee were elected. Advocate Rajendra K. Sail and Dr. Binayak Sen were unanimously elected as President and General Secretary respectively.

The first meeting of the State Council held on 29th March took stock of the deteriorating human rights situation in the state, and resolved to defend democracy with all its might. A two-pronged strategy was chalked out, which included expansion of the membership base with the formation of district level units, and challenging all forms of human rights violations in the established forums like the High Court to State Assembly, etc.

Specific issues identified for immediate response are to mobilize public opinion and forge the broadest possible alliance of democratic forces in the state to oppose Prevention of Terrorism Act, 2002 (POTA) that is being thrust upon the people of Chhattisgarh by the newly installed BJP government. Campaign would be carried out to pressurize the legislators and parliamentarians to stand up against this draconian legislation built on the patterns of The Rowlett Act passed by the British India in 1919, and the American Law on terrorism called 'Patriot' in the wake of September 11 disaster in New York in 2002.

PUCL has also decided to appeal to the Chhattisgarh Government to appoint a retired judge of the High Court as the Chairperson of the State Human Rights Commission instead of a retired police official, as at present. Failing which it would challenge the unprecedented step in the Chhattisgarh High Court. PUCL has pointed out that this was the only state in the country that had appointed a retired police official at this prestigious post, thus deliberately undermining the importance and effectiveness of a statutory body acting as a watchdog of the human rights situation in the state.

Expressing grave concern at the undue delay in the Shaheed Shanker Guha Niyogi Murder Trial, the PUCL has demanded that the Central and State governments take immediate and adequate steps to speed up the Murder Trial, and to see that justice is done by bringing the culprits to book. It shall carry out a signature campaign for speedy trial at the Supreme Court of India, and submit the same to the President of India.

PUCL has demanded setting up of a high-level independent Committee to review and accordingly recommend withdrawal of criminal cases pending against the political and social activists in Chhattisgarh. It also condemns the use of Black Laws like the National Security Act, Zilabadar Act, etc. against common citizens. According to PUCL, these are age-old repressive methods employed by the party in power against those who differ in thought and action from their policies and programmes.

PUCL would conduct independent citizen's investigations into the reported cases of encounter deaths in Sarguja, and submit its findings to the National Human Rights Commission for appropriate action.

PUCL takes a serious note of the undue and criminal delay in appointing the full-quota of judges at the Chhattisgarh High Court at Bilaspur. It would carry out a signature campaign among the various people's organisations, NGOs, prominent citizens, etc. and submit a memorandum in this regard to the Chief Justice of India.

PUCL has also expressed concern at the growing attacks on minorities in the state, especially in the name of curbing the so-called 'conversion by Christian missionaries' by the Sangh Parivar. The BJP government's plans to utilize the state apparatus to curb religious freedom and minority rights guaranteed under the Indian Constitution, which will be vehemently opposed by the PUCL by mobilizing secular and democratic forces in the state.

The campaign for the Right to Food would be streamlined by PUCL in the wake of recent reports of deaths due to malnutrition in Dantewada district of Chhattisgarh.

The PUCL report in this regard will be submitted to the Supreme Court of India when the already pending PUCL's Writ Petition comes up for hearing. Chhattisgarh PUCL plans to collect the nutritional data in these villages (Bargum of Kuakonda Block, Hidpal of Geedam Block, and Burgum-Mootanpal in Killepal village, which would be further submitted to the Commissioner appointed by the Supreme Court of India in this connection.

During the forthcoming Lok Sabha elections, PUCL would keep a close watch over the proceedings by inviting national observers, collect and analyse the affidavits submitted by the candidates of various political parties, and make public the information. - *Rajendra K. Sail, President*

RESOLUTIONS

The Chhattisgarh State branch of People's Union for Civil Liberties (PUCL) adopted the following Resolutions at its Convention held on 28th March 2004 at Town Hall, Raipur, Chhattisgarh:

Prevention of Terrorism Act (POTA)

The PUCL is deeply disturbed by the announcement of the BJP Government in Chhattisgarh about its intentions to implement Prevention of Terrorism Act (POTA) in the state of Chhattisgarh. The PUCL opposes the implementation of POTA to protect the democratic traditions, prevent fascism from redefining the basic tenets of our Constitution, and hijacking terms like 'nationalism' and 'patriotism'.

Coming in the wake of September 11 incident in New York, USA, POTA is nothing but a carbon copy of the American Law on Terrorism called 'PATRIOT'. In letter and spirit, it is a draconian preventive detention law, which reverses the burden of proof, and permits wicked forms of harassment of political opponents, especially of those who express dissent to globalization and fascism.

The PUCL is convinced that jumping on the American bandwagon of so-called 'war against terrorism', the BJP-led NDA government seized the opportunity to launch a newer and harsher version of TADA primarily to beat the minorities and its political opponents. While the US-inspired global agenda against 'terrorism' is primarily to prevent the landslide in economy, the Indian version of fighting terrorism in the form of POTA is part of the larger agenda of the Sangh Parivar for establishing Hindu Rashtra.

The past experience of two years has established that not only POTA has strengthened the repressive wing of the state, and trampled on all forms of democratic dissent, it is yet another step in terrorising minorities and secular-democratic organisations to the dictates of the emerging Hindu Fascist State.

During the past two years, it has been extended to all secular-democratic activities, and attacks on the interests of global capital are also classified as terrorist attacks.

The PUCL would strive to ensure that no one in a civilized democratic society be subject to such a law empowering the State to force any citizen to police custody for no reason at all. The PUCL would work to organize public opinion and mobilize democratic forces to oppose POTA by pressurizing our legislators and parliamentarians to stand up against this draconian legislation.

State Human Rights Commission

The PUCL is alarmed at the unprecedented step taken by the Chhattisgarh Government in appointing a retired police official as the Chairperson of the State Human Rights Commission.

Chhattisgarh is the only state where a retired police official holds such a prestigious post, while the Law of the Land clearly advocates appointment of a retired judge of the High Court to head the State Human Rights Commission.

The PUCL believes that such a move not only violates the letter and spirit of the Protection of Human Rights Act, 1993 but also raises doubts about the real motives of the Government. By departing from such a guideline, the Chhattisgarh Government has tried to deliberately undermine the importance and effectiveness of a statutory body acting as a watchdog on the human rights situation in the State.

We demand that the Chhattisgarh Government rectify this gross error and appoint a retired judge of the High Court as the Chairperson of the State Human Rights Commission.

Shaheed Shanker Guha Niyogi Murder Trial

The PUCL expresses grave concern at the undue delay in the Shaheed Shanker Guha Niyogi Murder Trial, now pending at the Hon'ble Supreme Court of India, after the Appeal has been admitted against the order of the High Court of Madhya Pradesh at Jabalpur in October 1998.

The lackluster manner in which the case is being pursued by the Central and State Governments demonstrates lack of political will on the part of the leadership to bring to book the culprits of the heinous crime committed by murdering the popular leader of a mass based democratic organisation in Chhattisgarh.

The PUCL believes that millions of people, along with various people's organisations, political parties, NGOs, intelligentsia, prominent citizens, etc., are awaiting the outcome of this Murder Trial and are concerned that justice should not only be done, but seen to be done. The PUCL demands that the NDA Government at the Centre and the Chhattisgarh Government led by Bhartiya Janata Party take immediate and adequate steps to speed up the Shaheed Niyogi Murder Trial, and to see that bringing to book the culprits does justice.

The PUCL should also carry out a concerted campaign for speedy trial at the Supreme Court of India. The PUCL should carry out a signature campaign beginning at the grassroots level, and submit the same to the President of India.

Review and Withdrawal of Criminal Cases against Political and Social Activists

The PUCL views with growing concern the State Government's total apathy and silence over the demands for the review and withdrawal of criminal cases pending against the political and social activists in Chhattisgarh. The people's hopes and aspirations after the formation of the state of Chhattisgarh in November 2000 included respectable and reasonable treatment of the political and social activists who are very often the target of powers that be for their democratic actions against the governments.

The filing of criminal cases and also the use of Black Laws like the NSA, Zilabadar Act, etc. are age old methods employed by the governments in power against those who differ in thought and action from their policies and programmes.

The PUCL appeals to the Chhattisgarh Government to set up a high-level independent Committee to review all such criminal cases against the political and social activists in the state and, subsequently, withdraw these cases. Special mention needs to be made about the criminal cases pending against the leaders of the Chhattisgarh Mukti Morcha, Communist Party of India, Ekta Parishad, Chhattisgarh Mahila Jagriti Sangathan, etc.

Appointment of High Court Judges

The PUCL expresses concern at the undue and criminal delay in appointing the full quota of Judges at the Chhattisgarh High Court at Bilaspur. The continued vacancies on the Hon'ble High Court negate the very spirit of jurisprudence that guarantees justice to every citizen. The non-appointment of Judges at the Chhattisgarh High Court amounts to denial of justice to the thousands of litigants whose hopes and aspirations had been raised with the formation of the separate State of Chhattisgarh.

The manner in which the cases are piling up at the Chhattisgarh High Court, primarily in the absence of adequate number of judges, is slowly but systematically corroding the common citizen's confidence in justice system.

Thus, the PUCL appeals to the concerned authorities, including the Chief Justice of India, to fill in the vacancies of judges on the Chhattisgarh High Court at Bilaspur without further delay.

Attacks on Minorities and Secular-democratic Polity

The PUCL expresses concern at the growing attacks on minorities in the State, especially in the name of curbing the so-called 'Conversion by Christian Missionaries' by the Sangh Parivar. The coming to power of the BJP in the State has also given credence to the belief that the state apparatus will be used to curb the religious freedom and minority rights guaranteed under the Indian Constitution.

The PUCL would strive to forge broadest possible alliance of secular and democratic forces in the states and carry out a campaign to strengthen the secular-democratic polity in the state.

POLITICS OF CHHATTISGARH

The key political players in Chhattisgarh state in central India are the ruling Bharatiya Janata Party, Indian National Congress, Janta Congress Chhattisgarh and Bahujan Samaj Party.

National politics

There are 11 Lok Sabha (lower house of the Indian Parliament) constituencies in Chhattisgarh.

State politics

The Chhattisgarh Legislative Assembly has 91 seats out of which 90 are directly elected from single-seat constituencies and 1 is nominated.

4

Language and Literature

LANGUAGE

Chhattisgarhi is the form of Hindi language or the language in its own right that is spoken and understood by majority of people in Chhattisgarh, but a total of 93 languages are spoken in the state, representing all three of India's major linguistic groups, Munda (Austro-Asiatic languages), Dravidian and Indo-European. All dialects use the Hindi script irrespective of the language group to which they belong. Chhattisgarhi is majorly an Indo-European dialect/language but has an abundance of Munda and Dravidian words and features.

Since Sanskritized Khari Boli or Hindi is the language of India (and Chhattisgarh) for official use like recruitment, education and there is lack of local people (at least from all ethno-language groups) in the state/local administration; there is ongoing change in the liguistic profile of the state accelerated with more interaction with outside world and desire to get developed.

In northern Chhattisgarh, dialects from all these three language groups are in use today; in middle part of Chhattisgarh, only Indo-European dialects have survived; and in southern

Chhattisgarh, Dravidian and Indo-European dialects are in use. According to H.L. Shukla- Munda dialects are progressing to the stage of becoming extinct; among Dravidian dialects, Parji is also facing extinction problem, Kurukh (Oraon) and Gondi are struggling; and IndoEropean dialects are in the process of losing their identity.

Munda Language Family

According to 1971 census of India, Korku was the major Munda dialects spoken by more than 200,000 people (It is not clear whether this count is for whole India or is specific to Chhattisgarh). Korku, Kharia and Korba are major Munda dialects in use in Chhattisgarh.

Other than these three, Muasi, Toori (in Raigarh), Nihali-Mankari, Khaerwari, Birhord, Kodaku (Sarguja), Dhelki, Mahto, Kora-Majhi, Munda, Mundari and Santhali are other Munda dialects spoken in Chhattisgarh which are either sub-dialects of above stated three dialects or are in the stage of extinction.

Dravidian Language Family

According to 1971 census of India, Kurukh or Oraon was mother-tongue of 300,609 people in Chhattisgarh and there were around 30,000 speakers of Parja or Dhurbi.

Gondi is the Dravidian language spoken by Gond tribals who call themselves Koitor or Koitol and therefore H.L. Shukla has called their language Koitor and has kept Dormi, Dandami-Maria, Bhuria, Abujh-Maria, Koya, Ghotul-muriya and others under this language. According to 1961 census of India, there were 3,900,000 Koitor or Gond tribals in India. Two thirds of these Gond/Koitor tribals are distributed over Madhya Pradesh and Chhattisgarh according to 1971 census. As of now, almost more than half of these tribals use the dialects (other than Koitor) in use in their respective areas. (Near Bhopal (capital of Madhyapradesh) which was once the stronghold of Koitor people, one cannot hear Koitor dialect in the circumference of 100 Kms).

Indo-European Language Family

Among 93 dialects spoken in Chhattisgarh, 70 are classified as belonging to this family. Under Chhattisgarhi group, the dialects spoken by Agariya, Binjhwari, Baigani, Bhuliya, Lariya, Dhanwar, Panka, Dindwar and many other tribals are included. Sadri is the dialect understood by many of the different tribal groups (Sadri is the name given to the Indo-European dialect which is adopted by tribal groups when they do not use their own dialect)—Sadri is in use from Chhattisgarh and Orissa to West-Bengal.

Similarly Halbi is understood by many of the different tribal groups in southern Chhattisgarh (earlier there were many different opinions about the language family of Halbi, but now it is usually accepted as an Indo-European dialect) - in 1951 census, it was found that more than 99% of Halbi speakers can speak at-least two dialects.

CHHATTISGARHI LANGUAGE

Chhattisgarhi is an Indo-Aryan language spoken in the Indian state of Chhattisgarh, by 24 million people. It is an Eastern Hindi language and is part of the Central Indo-Ayran language family with heavy vocabulary and linguistic features from Munda and Dravidian languages. Chhattisgarhi is also known as Dakshin Kosali and Dakshin Hindi as in ancient times Chhattisgarh was in the region Dakshina Kosala region of ancient India.

Chhattisgarhi has been known by the name Khaltahi to surrounding hill-people and by the name Laria to speakers in neighboring regions of Odisha to Chhattisgarh. The speakers are concentrated in the Indian state of Chhattisgarh and in adjacent areas of Madhya Pradesh, Odisha, and Jharkhand. Chhattisgarhi cultural and political movements, with origins from the 1920s, affirmed Chhattisgarhi linguistic and cultural identity and sought greater autonomy within India. It was 1 November, 2000 when 16 districts in the state of Madhya Pradesh became the new state of Chhattisgarh.

Classification

Chhattisgarhi is most closely related to other Kosali group of languages known as Bagheli and Awadhi (Avadhi), and these languages are classified in the East Central Zone of the Indo-Aryan languages or Kosali Language Group, the Indian branch of the Indo-European language family.

Its precise relationship to Hindi is complex and as with other members of the Hindustani dialect continuum, its status as a dialect or separate language is to some degree a judgment call.

According to the Indian Government, Chhattisgarhi is an eastern dialect of Hindi, but it is classified as a separate language in Ethnologue.

Chhattisgarhi has five different main dialects on the basis of geographical division:

1. Kedri (Central) Chhattisgarhi: This is purest form Chhattisgarhi, which is spoken in most of the Mahanadi Basin. Kedri Chhattisgarhi is uninfluenced by any other languages except Hindi. Mostly spoken in Bilaspur, Durg, Bemetara, Raipur, Rajnandgaon, Dhamtari, Kanker district of Chhattisgarh.
2. Utti (Eastern) Chhattisgarhi:Utti Chhattisgarhi, also known as Laria, is mostly spoken in Raigarh, Mahasamund, Gariaband, Raipur district of Chhattisgarh.
3. Budati / Khaltahi (Western) Chhattisgarhi: Marathi-language influence can be seen in Khaltahi Chhattisgarhi. Mostly spoken in Balaghat (Madhya Pradesh) and Kabirdham, Bemetara district of Chhattisgarh.
4. Bhandar (Northern) Chhattisgarhi: Also known as Sargujia Chhattisgarhi, it is mostly spoken in Koria, Surajpur, Sarguja, Jashpur, Balrampur district of Chhattisgarh.
5. Rakshahun (Southern) Chhattisgarhi: Mostly spoken in Dandkaranya region (Bastar) of Chhattisgarh. Godi and Halbi are other dialects which are widely spoken.

Vocabulary

Eastern Hindi dialects consist of Chhattisgarhi, Awadhi and Bagheli. All three dialects are closely related to each other. Chhattisgarhi, due to its heavy indigenous vocabulary and grammar, has always been treated as a distinct language. Awadhi and Bagheli are very closely associated with each other, Bagheli due to its regional association from Baghelkhandare considered as different dialects, otherwise it is considered a southern form of Awadhi.

Dialects

In addition to Chhattisgarhi Proper, the dialects of Chhattisgarhi are Baighani, Bhulia, Binjhwari, Kalanga, Kavardi, Khairagarhi, Sadri Korwa, and Surgujia. Surgujia is considered by some to be a distinct language.

Writing

Chhattisgarhi, like Hindi, is written using the Devanagari script, although it used to be written using the Odia script.

Chhattisgarhi Language Day

Chhattisgarhi Language Day (Chhattisgarhi Diwas) is celebrated every year on November 28 across the Indian states of Chhattisgarh. This day is regulated by the State Government.

Film industry

After the formation of the new state, films in Chhattisgarhi attracted artists everywhere around India. World-renowned vocalist Lata Mangeshkar and many others have sung songs in Chhattisgari. As the film industry is growing at a fast pace, it is now popularly known as Chhollywood.

5

Geography and Flora & Fauna

GEOGRAPHY

The northern and southern parts of the state are hilly, while the central part is a fertile plain. The highest point in the state is the Gaurlata. Deciduous forests of the Eastern Highlands Forests cover roughly 44% of the state. The state animal is the *van bhainsa*, or wild asian buffalo. The state bird is the *pahari myna*, or hill myna. The state tree is the Sal (Sarai) found in Bastar division.

Sal- The State Tree of Chhattisgarh

In the north lies the edge of the great Indo-Gangetic plain. The Rihand River, a tributary of the Ganges, drains this area. The eastern end of the Satpura Range and the western edge of the Chota Nagpur Plateau form an east-west belt of hills that divide the Mahanadi River basin from the Indo-Gangetic plain. The outline of Chhattisgarh is like a sea horse.

The central part of the state lies in the fertile upper basin of the Mahanadi river and its tributaries. This area has extensive rice cultivation. The upper Mahanadi basin is separated from the upper Narmada basin to the west by the Maikal Hills (part of the Satpuras) and from the plains of Odisha to the east by ranges of hills. The southern part of the state lies on the Deccan plateau, in the watershed of the Godavari River and its tributary, the Indravati River. The Mahanadi is the chief river of the state. The other main rivers are Hasdo (a tributary of Mahanadi), Rihand, Indravati, Jonk, Arpa and Shivnath. It is situated in the east of Madhya Pradesh.

The natural beauty of Koriya in Chhattisgarh includes dense forests, mountains, rivers and waterfalls. Koriya was a princely state during the British rule in India. Koriya is also known for the rich mineral deposits. Coal is found in abundance in this part of the country. The dense forests are rich in wildlife.

The Amrit Dhara Waterfall, Koriya's main attraction, is a natural waterfall which originates from the Hasdo River. The fall is situated at a distance of seven kilometres from Koriya. The waterfall is ideally located on the Manendragarh-Baikunthpur road. The Amrit Dhara Waterfall falls from a height of 27 m. The waterfall is about 3–4.5 m wide. The point where the water falls to the ground, a cloudy atmosphere is formed all around. Chirimiri is one of the more popular places, known for its pristine beauty, and healthy climate in Chhattisgarh.

Climate

The climate of Chhattisgarh is tropical. It is hot and humid because of its proximity to the Tropic of Cancer and its dependence on the monsoons for rains. Summer temperatures in Chhattisgarh can reach 45 °C (113 °F). The monsoon season is from late June to October and is a welcome respite from the heat. Chhattisgarh receives an average of 1,292 millimetres (50.9 in) of rain. Winter is from November to January and it is a good time to visit Chhattisgarh. Winters are pleasant with low temperatures and less humidity.

MAJOR CITIES

Largest cities in Chhattisgarh

(2011 Census of India estimate)

Rank	City	District	Population
1	Raipur	Raipur	4,063,872
2	Bhilai-Durg	Durg	3,343,872
3	Bilaspur	Bilaspur	2,663,629
4	Rajnandgaon	Rajnandgaon	1,537,133
5	Raigarh	Raigarh	1,493,984
6	Korba	Korba	1,206,640
7	Ambikapur	Sarguja	2,359,886
8	Jagdalpur	Bastar	125,345
9	Chirmiri	Koriya	100,656
10	Dhamtari	Dhamtari	90,254

FLORA AND FAUNA IN CHHATTISGARH

Some distinct varieties of common birds are also found in Bastar. For instance, the Jungle Crow is pitch dark and slightly larger than the domestic crow. It has a heavy-duty bill and a deep and hoarse "caw."

It is more audacious in attacking the nests of gentler birds and even the pups of smaller animals. Its movement in the forest often leads to tiger or panther kills.

Other species of avifauna include partridges (which nest in shrubs outside villages and run almost as fast as they fly), cattle egret, pond heron, babblers, parrots and parakeets, blue jay, wagtails, quails (both black and grey varieties), bulbul, koel , fly catchers, woodpeckers, sun bird and weaver bird.

Major wildlife species include blue bull, Chinkara, black buck, Sambhar, Barking Deer, wild dog, wild boar, jackals, hyena, and crocodiles. Tigers are in the Kurandi reserve forest and in the Kanger Valley National Park. Panthers are distributed almost all over Bastar, especially in the Northern plains. Indian sloth bears are in the Northern plains around Kanker and in the Southern part around Bailadila. Bison are in the Kutru National Park. Crocodiles are in the riverine ponds in the Kanger Valley National Park at Bhaisa-darha.

WILDLIFE OF CHHATTISGARH

The green Indian state of Chhattisgarh boasts a total of 3 National Parks and 11 Wildlife Sanctuaries known for their exceptional natural beauty and the unique and diverse flora and fauna.

Indravati National Park

Indravati National Park is the finest and most famous wildlife parks of Chhattisgarh. Also the only Tiger Reserve in the state, Indravati National Park is located in Dantewada district of Chhattisgarh. The Park derives its name from the Indravati River. With a total area of approximately 2799.08 sq km, Indravati attained the status of a National Park in 1981 and a Tiger Reserve in 1983 under the famous Project Tiger of India to become one of the most famous tiger reserves of India. The flora in the Indravati National Park is mainly comprises of tropical moist and dry deciduous type with predominance of the Sal, Teak and Bamboo trees. There are also rich patches of excellent grasslands providing much required fodder to Wild buffalos, Chital, Barking Deer, Nilgai, Gaurs and other herbivores of the park. The most commonly found trees in the park are Teak, Lendia, Salai, Mahua, Tendu, Semal, Haldu, Ber and Jamun. The major wildlife in Indravati National Park include the endangered Wild Buffalos, Barasinghas, Tigers, Leopards, Gaurs (Indian Bison), Nilgai,

Sambar, Chausingha (four-horned Antelope), Sloth Bear, Dhole (Wild Dog), Striped Hyena, Muntjac, Wild Boar, Flying Squirrel, Porcupine, Pangolins, Monkeys and Langurs among many others. The commonly found reptiles in the park are Freshwater Crocodile, Monitor Lizard, Indian Chameleon, Common Krait, Indian Rock Python, Cobra and Russell's Viper to name a few. The Park also gives shelter to the large variety of birds of which Hill Maina is the most important species here.

Kanger Valley National Park

Located amidst the 34 km long and scenic Kanger Valley, a Biosphere Reserve, Kanger Valley National Park is one of the most beautiful and picturesque national parks of India. The beautiful park is located on the banks of Kholaba River at a distance of about 27 km from Jagdalpur (headquarter of Bastar). Spread over an area of approximately 200 sq km comprising mainly of hilly terrain, the Park derives its name from the Kanger River, which flows throughout its length.

Known for its scenic beauty and the unique and rich biodiversity, Kanger Valley attained the status of a National Park in 1982. Besides wildlife and plants, there are many tourist attractions inside the park such as the Kutamsar Caves, Kailash Caves, Dandak Caves and Tiratgarh Waterfalls. Kanger Dhara and Bhaimsa Dhara (a Crocodile Park) are the two beautiful and exotic picnic resorts in the Park.

The flora in the park chiefly comprises of mixed moist deciduous type of forests with predominance of Sal, Teak and Bamboo trees. In fact, the Kanger Valley is the only region in the Peninsular India where one of the last pockets of virgin and untouched forests still left.

Major Wildlife of the Kanger Valley National Park are the Tigers, Leopards, Mouse Deer, Wild Cat, Chital, Sambar, Barking Deer, Jackals, Langurs, Rhesus Macaque, Sloth Bear, Flying Squirrel, Wild Boar, Striped Hyena, Rabbits, Pythons, Cobra, Crocodiles, Monitor Lizards and Snakes to name a few. The avian fauna at the Park includes Hill Myna, Spotted Owlet,

Red Jungle Fowls, Racket-tailed Drongos, Peacocks, Parrots, Steppe Eagles, Red Spur Fall, Phakta, Bhura Teeter, Tree Pie and Heron among many others.

Sanjay National Park

Located in Surguja and KOdia districts of Chhattisgarh, Sanjay National Park is one of the most important wildlife sanctuaries in central India. Also known as Ghasi Das National Park (in Chhattisgarh), the sanctuary is famous for its rich and diverse flora and fauna and attained the status of a National Park in 1981. Sanjay National Park covers an area of approximately 2,303 sq km and is well drained by a number of rivers, rivulets and other perennial sources of water, providing enough water supply for the for the wildlife and birds. Sanjay National Park houses a wide variety of wildlife and birds including some of the rare and endangered species and has great potential to emerge as one of the finest wildlife destinations in central India.

The flora in Sanjay National Park chiefly comprises of mixed forests dominated with Sal and extensive patches of Bamboo forests. Other major plants in the sanctuary include Salai, Dhawada (Anogeissus latifolia), Palas (Butea monosperma), Gurajan (Lania choromendelica), Semal, Mahua, Harra, Haldu, Ber and Tendu.

The rich and diverse vegetation supports a wide variety of wildlife in the Park. The major wildlife found in Sanjay National Park includes Tigers, Leopards, Chital, Nilgai, Chinkara, Jackals, Sambar, Four-horned Antelopes, Jungle Cat, Barking Deer, Porcupine, Monkey, Bison, Striped Hyena, Sloth Bear, Wild Dogs, Wild Pigs, Cobra, Monitor Lizards, Python to name a few.

Sanjay National Park is also a little paradise for bird lovers and houses wide varieties of avian population with prominent being the Parrots, Peacock, Bulbul, Minivets Orioles, Wagtails, Munias, Blue Kingfisher, Phakta, Ducks, Neelkanth Pigeon, Dabchick, Peafowl, Crimson Breasted Barbet, Teetar, Tree Pie,

Racket-tailed Drongos, Egrets, and Herons to name few. A visit to Sanjay National Park promises to be an exciting and rewarding experience for all wildlife enthusiasts and nature lovers.

Barnawapara Wildlife Sanctuary

Located in northern part of Mahasamund district of Chhattisgarh, Barnawapara Wildlife Sanctuary is one of the finest and important wildlife sanctuaries in the region. Established in 1976 under Wildlife Protection Act of 1972, the sanctuary is relatively a small one covering an area of only 245 sq km. The Barnawapara Wildlife Sanctuary is known for its lush green vegetations and unique wildlife. The flora of Barnawapara Wildlife Sanctuary chiefly comprises of tropical dry deciduous forest with Teak, Sal, Bamboo and Terminalia being the prominent trees. Other major plants found in the sanctuary include Semal, Mahua, Ber and Tendu. The rich and lush vegetation cover supports a wide variety of wildlife in the sanctuary. The major wildlife of the Barnawapara Sanctuary include Tigers, Sloth Bear, Flying Squirrels, Jackals, Four-horned Antelopes, Leopards, Chinkara, Black Buck, Jungle Cat, Barking Deer, Porcupine, Monkey, Bison, Striped Hyena, Wild Dogs, Chital, Sambar, Nilgai, Gaur, Muntjac, Wild Boar, Cobra, Python to name a few. The sanctuary also has a sizable bird population with prominent being the Parrots, Bulbul, White-rumped Vultures, Green Avadavat, Lesser Kestrels, Peafowl, Wood Peckers, Racket-tailed Drongos, Egrets, and Herons to name few.

Sitanandi Wildlife Sanctuary

Located in Dhamtari district of Chhattisgarh, Sitanadi Wildlife Sanctuary is one of the most famous and important wildlife sanctuaries in central India. Established in 1974 under Wildlife Protection Act of 1972, the sanctuary covers an area of approximately 556 sq km, comprising of highly undulating and hilly terrain with altitudes ranging between 327-736 mts. The beautiful sanctuary derives its name from the Sitanadi River that originates in the middle of sanctuary and joins Mahanadi

River near Deokhut. Sitanadi Wildlife Sanctuary is known for its lush green flora and rich and unique and diverse fauna and has great potential to emerge as one of the finest wildlife destinations in central India.

The flora in Sitanadi Wildlife Sanctuary chiefly comprises of moist peninsular Sal, Teak and Bamboo forests. Other major plants in the sanctuary include Semal, Mahua, Harra, Ber and Tendu. The rich and lush vegetation cover supports a wide variety of wildlife in the sanctuary. The major wildlife found in Sitanadi Sanctuary include Tigers, Leopards, Flying Squirrels, Jackals, Four-horned Antelopes, Chinkara, Black Buck, Jungle Cat, Barking Deer, Porcupine, Monkey, Bison, Striped Hyena, Sloth Bear, Wild Dogs, Chital, Sambar, Nilgai, Gaur, Muntjac, Wild Boar, Cobra, Python among many others. The sanctuary also has a sizable bird population with prominent being the Parrots, Bulbul, Peafowl, Pheasant, Crimson Breasted Barbet, Teetar, Tree Pie, Racket-tailed Drongos, Egrets, and Herons to name few. Sitanadi Sanctuary is also being prepared to develop it as an important tiger sanctuary in the region.

6

Economy

ECONOMY

Chhattisgarh's nominal gross state domestic product (GSDP) is estimated at 3.26 lakh crore (US$45 billion) in 2018–19, the 17th largest state economy in India. The economy of Chhattisgarh recorded a growth rate of 6.7% in 2017–18.Chhattisgarh's success factors in achieving high growth rate are growth in agriculture and industrial production.

Tea production

Chhattisgarh State is ranked as the 17th-largest tea-producing state in India. The districts of Jashpur and Surguja are favourable tea production areas. In Jashpur district, the first tea plantation, Brahmnishthajaya Sogara Ashram was established under the direction of Pujya Pad Gurupad.

Tea production started after two years at the Sogara Ashram. A tea processing unit was established in Sogara Ashram and the unit name set as the Aghor Tea Processing Plant. The forestry department has also started a tea plantation motivated by the Sogara Ashram.

In Surguja district, a tea nursery is being developed by the Margdarshan Sansthan Agriculture College in Ambikapur, Surguja.

AGRICULTURE

Agriculture is counted as the chief economic occupation of the state. According to a government estimate, net sown area of the state is 4.828 million hectares and the gross sown area is 5.788 million hectares. Horticulture and animal husbandry also engage a major share of the total population of the state. About 80% of the population of the state is rural and the main livelihood of the villagers is agriculture and agriculture-based small industry.

The majority of the farmers are still practising the traditional methods of cultivation, resulting in low growth rates and productivity. The farmers have to be made aware of modern technologies suitable to their holdings. Providing adequate knowledge to the farmers is essential for better implementation of the agricultural development plans and to improve the productivity.

Chloroxylon is used for Pest Management in Organic Rice Cultivation in Chhattisgarh, India

Considering this and a very limited irrigated area, the

productivity of not only rice but also other crops is low, hence the farmers are unable to obtain economic benefits from agriculture and it has remained as subsistence agriculture till now.

Medicinal Rice of Chhattisgarh used as Immune Booster

Herbal Farming in Chhattisgarh: Aloe vera

Herbal Farming in Chhattisgarh: Gulbakawali

Herbal Farming in Chhattisgarh: Safed Musli with Arhar

Agricultural products

The main crops are rice, maize, *kodo-kutki* and other small millets and pulses (*tuar* and *kulthi*); oilseeds, such as groundnuts (peanuts), soybeans and sunflowers, are also grown. In the mid-1990s, most of Chhattisgarh was still a monocrop belt. Only one-fourth to one-fifth of the sown area was double-cropped. When a very substantial portion of the population is dependent on agriculture, a situation where nearly 80% of a state's area is covered only by one crop, immediate attention to turn them into double crop areas is needed. Also, very few cash crops are grown in Chhattisgarh, so there is a need to diversify the agriculture produce towards oilseeds and other cash crops. Chhattisgarh is also called the "rice bowl of central India".

Kodo Millet is used as Life Saving Medicine in Chhattisgarh, India

Bastar Beer prepared from Sulfi

Irrigation

In Chhattisgarh, rice, the main crop, is grown on about 77% of the net sown area. Only about 20% of the area is under irrigation; the rest depends on rain. Of the three agroclimatic zones, about 73% of the Chhattisgarh plains, 97% of the Bastar plateau and 95% of the northern hills are rainfed. The irrigated area available for double cropping is only 87,000 ha in Chhattisgarh plains and 2300 ha in Bastar plateau and northern hills. Due to this, the productivity of rice and other crops is low, hence the farmers are unable to obtain economic benefits from agriculture and it has remained as subsistence agriculture till now, though agriculture is the main occupation of more than 80% of the population.

In Chhattisgarh region, about 22% of net cropped area was under irrigation as compared to 36.5% in Madhya Pradesh in 1998–99, whereas the average national irrigation was about 40%. The irrigation is characterised by a high order of variability ranging from 1.6% in Bastar to 75.0% in Dhamtari. Based on an average growth trend in the irrigated area, about 0.43% additional area is brought under irrigation every year as compared to 1.89% in Madhya Pradesh and 1.0% in the country as a whole. Thus, irrigation has been growing at a very low rate in Chhattisgarh and the pace of irrigation is so slow, it would take about 122 years to reach the 75% level of net irrigated area in Chhattisgarh at the present rate of growth.

Chhattisgarh has a limited irrigation system, with dams and canals on some rivers. Average rainfall in the state is around 1400 mm and the entire state falls under the rice agroclimatic zone. The Large variation in the yearly rainfall directly affects the production of rice. Irrigation is the prime need of the state for its overall development and therefore the state government has given top priority to development of irrigation.

A total of four major, 33 medium and 2199 minor irrigation projects have been completed and five major, 9 medium and 312 minor projects are under construction, as of 31 March 2006.

INDUSTRIAL SECTOR

Chhattisgarh has been famous for its rice mills, cements and steel plants. Durg, Raipur, Korba and Bilaspur are the leading districts in the field of industrial development in the state. Bhilai Steel Plant (BSP) in Durg district happens to be the largest integrated steel plant of the country. Establishment of BSP in 1950's led to development of a wide range of industries at Raipur and Bhilai. Raipur district has got the rare distinction of having the largest number of big and small-scale cement plants.

Bilaspur and Durg districts too are home to a number of large-scale cement plants korba, with a number of power generating units established by NTPC and MPEB, is among the leading power generation centres of the country. Aluminium and explosive plants are also located in Korba district. There are a number of industrial growth centres in the state which host hundreds of industrial units. The principal growth centres in the state are : Urla and Siltara (Raipur); Borai (Durg) and Sirgitti (Bilaspur).

Power sector

Chhattisgarh is one of the few states of India where the power sector is effectively developed. Based on the current production of surplus electric power, the position of the State is comfortable and profitable. The Chhattisgarh State Electricity

Board (CSEB) is in a strong position to meet the electricity requirement of the new state and is in good financial health. Chhattisgarh provides electricity to several other states because of surplus production.

In Chhattisgarh, National Thermal Power Corporation Limited (|NTPC) has Sipat Thermal Power Station with a capacity of 2,980 MW at Sipat, Bilaspur; LARA Super Thermal Power Station with a nameplate capacity of 1600MW and Korba Super Thermal Power Station with a capacity of 2,600 MW at Korba, while CSEB's units have a thermal capacity of 1,780 MW and hydel capacity of 130 MW. Apart from NTPC and CSEB, there are a number of private generation units of large and small capacity. The state government has pursued a liberal policy with regard to captive generation which has resulted in a number of private players coming up.

The state has a potential of 61,000 MW of additional thermal power in terms of availability of coal for more than 100 years and more than 2,500 MW hydel capacity. To use this vast potential, substantial additions to the existing generation capacity are already underway.

Steel sector

The steel industry is one of the biggest heavy industries of Chhattisgarh. Bhilai Steel Plant, Bhilai operated by SAIL, with a capacity of 5.4 million tonnes per year, is regarded as a significant growth indicator of the state. More than 100 steel rolling mills, 90 sponge iron plants and ferro-alloy units are in Chhattisgarh. Along with Bhilai, today Raipur, Bilaspur, Korba and Raigarh have become the steel hub of Chhattisgarh. Today, Raipur has become the centre of the steel sector, the biggest market for steel in India.

Aluminium sector

The aluminium industry of Chhattisgarh was established by Bharat Aluminium Company Limited, which has a capacity of around 600,000 tonnes each year.

NATURAL RESOURCES

Chhattisgarh is rich in mineral resources. Twenty per cent of the country's steel and cement is produced in the State. Iron-ore, limestone, dolomite, coal, bauxite are found in abundance. It is the only tin-ore producing state in the country. Other minerals such as korandum, garnet, quartz, marble, diamond are also found in Chhattisgarh. Compared to 1998-1999, the production of coal, iron ore and limestone registered an increase of 29,49 lakh tonnes, 13.40 lakh tonnes and 30.13 lakh tonnes respectively in 1999-2000. The revenue receipt from minerals in 2001-02 is likely to increase to Rs. 455 crore from Rs. 394.50 crore during the preceding year.

Forest

Forests occupy 41.33% of the total area (as per the latest report by the Indian Forest Service) and the rich forest resources include wood, tendu leaves, honey and lac. Approximately 3%is under very dense forest, 25.97% is moderately dense, 12.28% is open forest and 0.09% is scrub.

Flora of Kabirdham District

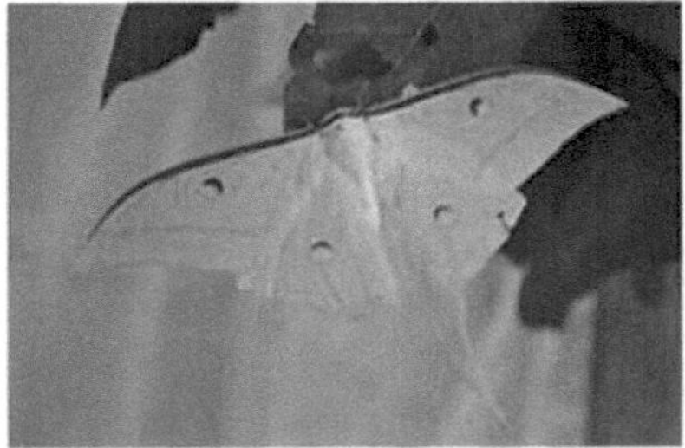

Indian Luna Moth in Chhattisgarh Forest

Ventilago in Biodiversity Rich Chhattisgarh Forest

Mahua

Mineral deposits

Chhattisgarh is rich in minerals. It produces 20% of the country's total cement produce. It has the highest output of coal in the country with second-highest reserves. It is third in iron ore production and first in tin production. Limestone, dolomite and bauxite are abundant. It is the only tin ore-producing state in India. Other commercially extracted minerals include corandum, garnet, quartz, marble, alexandrite and diamonds.

Maikal Hills in Chhattisgarh

Mineral Wealth from Chandidongri, Chhattisgarh

Information and technologies

In recent years, Chhattisgarh is also getting exposure in information technology (IT) projects and consultancy. Its government is also promoting IT and has set up a body to take care of the IT solutions. The body, known as CHiPS, is providing large IT projects such as Choice, Swan, etc.

Major companies

Major companies with a presence in the state include:

- Metal: Bhilai Steel Plant, Jindal Steel and Power, Bharat Aluminium Company
- Oil: Indian Oil Corporation, Hindustan Petroleum Corporation Limited
- Mining: NMDC, South Eastern Coalfields
- Power : NTPC, Lanco Infratech, KSK Energy Ventures, Jindal Power Limited

Exports

Chhattisgarh's total exports were US$353.3 million in 2009–10. Nearly 75% of exports comes from Bhilai and the remaining from Urla, Bhanpuri and Sirgitti. The major exports products include steel, handicrafts, handlooms, blended yarn, food and agri-products, iron, aluminium, cement, minerals and engineering products. CSIDC (Chhattisgarh State Industrial Development Corporation Limited) is the nodal agency of the Government of Chhattisgarh for export promotion in the state.

INVESTMENT AND INDUSTRIAL POLICIES

Mineral Policy-2001

Introduction: The State of Chhattisgarh was carved out of erstwhile Madhya Pradesh to provide deference to its distinctive historical, social background and natural resources. It is paradoxical that the State with richest natural endowments is amongst poor in the country. The basic purpose of its formation would be defeated if the natural resources are not used due to constraints of stringent forest laws and environment problems. To ease these strains and to provide accessibility in the benefit of natural resources utilization to the deprived class of the region, it has become imperative to evolve a suitable mineral policy for the nascent State.

MINERAL WEALTH

The geological and tectonic set up of the State is very conducive to provide many locales of minerals of different varieties. Almost 28 varieties of minerals have been reported in the State, most important being precious stone diamond, gold, iron ore, limestone, dolomite, tin ore, bauxite and coal.

The sole occurrence of tin ore in the country is reported from the State to the tune of 28.89 MT. in southern part of Bastar region. Iron ore contemplates to form backbone for industrialization of any State. At present, its small portion is being worked out and vast potential still remains to be utilized through export promotion and putting up steel manufacturing industries.

The world's best quality of iron ore is found in Bailadila deposits of Dantewara district. The other important deposits of iron ore are located in Kanker, Durg and Rajnandgaon districts. The State is endowed with its huge reserves to the tune of 1969 MT. At present NDMC is exploiting iron ore for export to Japan and catering to the needs of Vishakhapatnam Steel Plant. Dalli-Rajhara group of mines is being exploited by BSP for their Steel Plant at Bhilai. The bauxite ore of magic metal Aluminium is found abundantly in Surguja, Jashpur, Korba, Kawardha and Bastar region.

It can support export orientation unit in the State. At present, public undertaking company BALCO has exploited Phutka Pahar deposit and now the Manipat deposit is catering to the needs of BALCO through MPSMC for their aluminium plant at Korba.

The limestone deposits contribute a major share of mineral deposits in the State. It sustains 9 major cement plants with an installed capacity of 14.75 million tonnes and contributes to minor cement plants also. Cement grade limestone registered a significant presence in Raipur, Durg, Bilaspur, Bastar, Janjgir, Kawardha and Raigarh districts. The reserves to the tune of 3580.6 MT have been proved and vast area still remains to be explored. The low-grade limestone is used as building material abundantly.

The other important industrial mineral dolomite, which is mostly used in steel plants and refractories, is located in Bastar, Durg, Bilaspur and Janjgir districts and has total 606 MT reserves in the State. The largest share of mineral revenue is contributed by coal. It is being exploited and marketed by Coal India Ltd.

Diamond incidences in Manipur region of Raipur districts have been confirmed and 8 potential blocks qualify in the State for possible incidence of kimberlite, the mother rock of diamond.

Other minerals like corundum, clay, quartzite, fluorite, beryl, andalusite, kyanite, silliminite, talc, garnet, silica sand etc. are reported from the State. Rare precious minerals like alexandrite and kornerupine are also reported. Apart from these minerals vast reserves of granite of various attractive shades, which can be used as decorative stone, are also available.

INFRASTRUCTURE IN CHHATTISGARH FOR MINING ACTIVITY

Infrastructure Development Corporation has been constituted under the Chairmanship of Hon'ble Chief Minister of Chhattisgarh. Hence infrastructure constraints would be addressed speedily. Available infrastructure in the State are:-

Railways: It is a dominant factor for industrialization of the State. The State capital is linked to most of the Indian States and to major seaport by rail line network. This will help a long way for mineral movement in the State. However, linkages of Durg-Rajhara rail line with Jagdalpur and Anuppur - Vishrampur line with Ramnujganj via Ambikapur is available for transportation of mineral wealth and others.

Road Network: Chhattisgarh is well connected by road network. There are 3 National Highways passing through the State alongwith many State Highways connecting all district headquarters of the State.

Power: Power is a vital input for mineral based industries. The total installed capacity in the State is approx. 3900 MW. Efforts are being made to encourage entrepreneurs to develop their own captive power projects.

Human Resources: Looking at the number of mines and possibilities of up coming of many ore, a large number of technically qualified personnel's are required. Geology is taught in Universities at graduate and post-graduate levels. Many Engineering and Polytechnic Colleges and I.T.I Training Courses persist in the area. Chhattisgarh is well known for its labour potential for peaceful industrial atmosphere.

REGULATION OF MINES AND MINERALS

- Although mineral wealth vests with the State Government, yet the subject of regulation of Mines and Minerals Development is covered under 7th schedule of constitution of India. By virtue of this, the Parliament has exclusive power to make laws with respect to regulation of Mines and Mineral Development.
- Mines and Minerals (Regulation and Development) Act, 1957 (MMRD Act) has been enacted by Parliament and Mineral Concession Rules 1960 have been issued by the Central Government in exercise of power given under section 13 of this Act. The Central Government has also framed Mineral Conservation and Development Rules. 1988 for conservation and systematic development of minerals except coal, atomic minerals and minor minerals. Rule making powers in respect of minor minerals have been delegated to the States under section 15 of this Act.
- Procedures regarding legislation of minor minerals is contained in Madhya Pradesh Minor Mineral Rules 1996. As per rule 29 (5) the fixation of royalty rates and dead rents for minor minerals is vested with the State Government, who can not increase the royalty rates within three years of time.

According to Rule 56 the Mineral Administration royalty realization is vested with Gram Panchayats:

- A major milestone was achieved in mineral legislation and policy during 1999-2000 when the MMRD Act 1957 was amended to provide greater delegation of power to the State Government and has brought about major procedural simplifications.

- With the opening of India economy, Government of India have liberalized the grant of licences and leases for most of the minerals, except Atomic minerals and Fuel minerals under the National Mineral Policy of 1993. This policy envisages:
  (a) 13 Minerals *viz.* iron ore, manganese, chromite, sulphur, gold, diamond, copper, lead, zinc, molybdenum, tungsten, nickel and platinum group of minerals have been deleted from the list of minerals which had been earlier reserved for exploitation by the public sector, These minerals are now opened for exploitation by private sector.
  (b) Foreign investment and technology will be encouraged. Ceiling on foreign equity in the mining industry has been removed.
  (c) Limestone has been deleted from the list of scheduled minerals and no approval from Government of India is required before sanctioning leases for cement grade limestone.

Objectives

- To develop mineral resources keeping the priority for export oriented minerals, strategic minerals, base metals and to enhance the reserves of traditional minerals used by the local populace.
- In case of minerals like gold, base metals and diamond, where enormous capital outlay and modern technique are required for conducting aero-geophysical survey at 250 m. line interval/foreign participation will be sought,
- Ecological concerns shall be in conformity with the local ecosystem.
- The department has felt the need for development of existing laboratories like chemical, petrological, geophysical and photogeological laboratories with modern equipments and gadgets to increase the accuracy and quality of the mineral resources and their uses.

- To evolve suitable technology for further use of today's subgrade ore to meet further requirements, suitable beneficiation studies would be made with adequate R&D support.
- The existing policy of granite has failed to encourage the development of granite reserves in the State, which has immense potential for its development. Therefore, the State has proposed to adopt the Government of India, Granite Conservation and Development Rules, 1999.
- Mineral policy shall be in tune with maximum participation of the people in Mineral industries keeping the transaction transparent and to increase the mineral revenue.
- Effective measures to check illegal mining and pilferage of mineral revenue will be formulated.
- A continuous process of apprising technical staff with the latest techniques and instruments in mineral exploration and analysis round the year training programme has to be adhered to.

MINERAL EXPLORATION

Minerals are at the foundation of all human endeavours since the dawn of civilization. These are valuable natural resources and are non-replenishable and wasting assets. The search for additional mineral resources is, therefore, a compelling process in any developing country. This mineral search activity will have to maintain high degree of professionalism and commercial viable studies. The high risk and high gain character of exploration demand more careful approach in its planning and execution.

Mineral exploration is an inevitable and continuous process in the State., the Search for additional mineral resources will, therefore, be kept in pace with the industrial development of the State In the modern technology of high-grade environment, the intensity of mineral search has to be maintained to bring high degree of professionalism that would thrive on fundamental considerations of return on investment.

Mineral exploration work aims at resource generation. Every expenditure in exploration may not be result oriented. Hence to venture into exploration expenditure involve lot of risk. It is, therefore, proposed that such expenditure should be categorised under Research and Development expenditure of the State.

The main activity of the Directorate of Geology and Mining, Chhattisgarh has been mineral survey and prospecting. It includes to locate new mineral deposits and to evaluate the known deposits for their integrated development. Most of the minerals found on the surface have been located and exploited by conventional methods Now the target area has been shifted to remote areas and deep-seated mineral deposits.

This mineral search requires sophisticated technology. Aerial geophysical surveys at 250 metres line internal has to be carried out to locate mineral bearing zones based on anomalies. Stream sediment samples, rock samples and limited borehole samples have to be collected to narrow down the area of exploration. The analytical part of the sample has to be performed with extra precision to achieve the required end product. Therefore, a well equipped laboratory is essential to deliver the accurate quality analysis of mineral resources and their industrial uses. The existing chemical, petrological and photogeological laboratories would be equipped with modern equipment to provide logistic support to high tech entrepreneurs venturing in the State.

Beneficiation study of the subgrade ore, substitute study for scarce minerals and industrial use of small deposits will be undertaken.

Technical staff of the Directorate will be associated with any exportation venture conducted in the States other than Central Government and public undertakings.

Mineral investigations were, so far, carried out mainly to cater the demands of large industries. Hence, the smaller deposits were not given importance. Now, the detailed prospecting for the smaller deposits will also be carried out to explore their industrial uses. With the globalization of economy, mineral sector has also been opened up for private/foreign investment. Chhattisgarh State has immense potential for minerals to be exported. This being a high risk venture, the capital requirement is enormous. The nascent State like Chhattisgarh can not afford such bigger capital outlay. It is therefore, proposed to invite private/foreign investment in search for high value scarce minerals like :

- Diamond and gem stones
- Gold
- Base metals
- Tin
- Bauxite

The iron ore is being exported from Bailadila iron ore mines of Dantewara District. So, identification of areas for exporting investment explorations has been proposed for the following minerals:

- Diamond/gem stones
- Gold
- Base metals
- Iron-ore
- Granite
- Bauxite
- Tin-ore

Mineral exploration is a high risk venture. Hence, inflow of funds should facilitate in the endeavour exerting the least burden to the Government exchequer. Imposition of stringent self-serving restriction will disallow the Inflow of fund in this sector. The State has immense unexplored potential of mineral wealth which requires heavy capital outlay. The help of private funds and know-how has become inevitable. Therefore, State would adopt modus operandi to invite entrepreneurs to undertake such exploration works. This will facilitate unveiling of many important mineral locales in the State.

Small and isolated deposits of minerals are scattered all over the State. The economic exploitation through small scale mining can be undertaken to generate employment in the scheduled areas. Efforts should be made to promote small-scale mining in scientific and efficient manner safeguarding environment imperatives.

Besides the Directorate of Geology and Mining, there are various Central Government agencies engaged in mineral exploration in the State. Efforts will be made to achieve a proper coordination among these agencies to avoid duplication of efforts and to ensure optimum use of the resources. A special cell in the Directorate of Geology and Mining will be established to provide escort services.

The information regarding availability of minerals, exploration status, mining and setting up of mineral based industries shall be made available to the entrepreneurs. A special cell in the Directorate of Geology and Mining will be formed to undertake the following activities :-

Preparation of an inventory of minerals produced in the State and updating it regularly. The maps indicating area permitted for prospecting an mining leases will be prepared and be updated every year. Mineral beneficiation studies, will be made on productive use of mineral waste and mines to prevent adverse effect on environment, will be undertaken.

Brochures would be punished for target minerals like gemstones, cement grade limestone, granite, gold etc. These would facilitated setting up of mineral-based industries in the State.

IMPROVING COMPETITIVENESS OF SMALL SCALE INDUSTRIES

The Government has decided on a number of Initiatives for small-scale industries so that these industries can effectively leverage on their strengths and have long-term sustainable growth. This will be achieved by helping them enhance their competitiveness in a market driven economy through improved product quality, increased productivity and process innovation.

- *Project Preparation:* To address the issue of inadequate project preparation, the Government will adopt a three stage process:
  - Undertake I review through a professional agency, the investment potential survey for each district;
  - Prepare a shelf of bankable project reports in identified areas to be shared with local entrepreneurs;
  - Work closely with Financial Institutions for funding specific projects.
- *Use of Information Technology:* Although the cost of implementing IT solutions for improving productivity for an individual small scale unit may/be very high, groups of units can share such costs. Accordingly, the Government will help identify suitable IT applications, disseminate information and organise training with local Industry Associations and Non Government Organisations
- *Human Resource Development:* The State will promote specialised training institutes in public-private-partnership to cater to the specific needs of small scale industries, wherein infrastructure facilities will be provided by the Government with the management of the facility left to Industry Associations.
- *Collaborative Marketing:* The Government will support market promotion activities like buyer seller meets, trade fairs, etc., through active participation and organisation. Chhattisgarh State Industrial Development Corporation (CSIDC) will develop a comprehensive database to provide trade and export related information to local small scale enterprises. The Government will introduce a common purchase policy for purchase of items manufactured by small-scale enterprises of the State. In order to disseminate the necessary information on Government procurement, a booklet incorporating items required by State Government Corporations/Boards and large Companies will be published and put on the Internet. The Government will also assist the efforts of civil society

organisations which facilitate marketing of tiny/small scale industries products, especially in the rural areas.

- *Certification and Testing:* The Government will promote the setting up of a network of testing and certification facilities for the use of small scale industries, especially for those who wish to enter the export market. Specialised facilities often require large investments and the Government will support initiatives of the private sector for setting-up such testing and certification facilities. Purchase of ISO /ISI certified products produced by the small scale industries will be given preference for procurement by Government Departments / Undertakings of the State Government.
- *Working Capital:* To support the working capital requirements of small scale units, the Government will ensure payments against procurement from these units by State Government Departments/Undertakings of the State Government within a period of 10 days.

Directed Incentives : The package of incentives that the State will provide to catalyse industrial development will be directed towards:

- Thrust Industries;
- Mega Projects; and
- Small Scale Industries in thrust sectors

Additional incentives will be provided to industries that:

- Employ a large number of women workers;
- Are set up by Scheduled Tribes / Scheduled Castes; and
- Invest in quality control and innovation

These incentives shall be available to a New Industrial Unit set up after the date of enforcement of this industrial policy. Expansion and modernisation of existing units will be driven by business imperatives and not on account of incentives per se.

A special package for sick industries will be announced separately based on a detailed evaluation of the causes for industrial sickness. Recommendations for a liberal exit policy will be made to the Central Government for fundamentally sick industries that cannot be revived.

Thrust Industries including Export Oriented Units

- *Infrastructure Support:* Whenever industries are located in places other than designated industrial areas, the government will provide assistance to meet a part of the cost of developing infrastructure like land, power, water facilities, construction of approach roads, staff housing, etc., to medium and large industrial projects. This assistance will be to the extent of 25% of the— infrastructure cost subject to a maximum of Rs. 10 million (Rs.1 crore)
- *Electricity Duty:* All new units will be exempt from the payment of electricity duty for a period of 10 years from the date of commercial production
- *Commercial Tax:* Floor rate of Value Added Tax, as and when introduced

Mega Projects

- *Definition:* Industries with investments in fixed assets in excess of Rs.1 000 million (Rs. 100 crores) shall be considered as Mega Industries/Projects.
- *Infrastructure Support:* Whenever industries are located in places other than designated industrial areas, the Government will provide assistance to meet a part of the cost of developing infrastructure like land, power, water facilities, construction of approach roads, staff housing, etc., to Mega Industrial Projects (irrespective of whether they are in thrust sectors or not) coming up in the State. This assistance will be to the extent of 25% of the infrastructure cost subject to a maximum of Rs.20 million (Rs.2 crores).
- *Power:* Chhattisgarh is a power surplus State, and hence ordinarily there would be no need for captive power

generation. However, in case the project requires such uninterrupted power of definite quality that the Electricity Board would not be able to supply, captive power generation will be allowed for such industrial units. If the industry can generate power from waste heat recovery, it would be encouraged to set up a captive power plant.

- Such a unit with captive power generation would be allowed to wheel power directly to sister concerns, but not to any other party within the State. Chhattisgarh State Electricity Board (CSEB) would assist such captive power producers to sell their surplus power to other States, on the same terms and conditions as those of CSEB, while the rate of power purchase between CSEB and the captive power producer in such a sale would be finalised after mutual agreement.
- CSEB would purchase power from such captive power plants only when required by it, and the rate of such purchase would be decided after considering rates of all other power sources.
- *Electricity Duty:* All new units will be exempt from the payment of electricity duty for a period of 15 years from the date of commercial production
- *Sales Tax:* Sales tax deferment will be provided to new units for a period of 5 years subject to a maximum of 125% of the fixed capital investment

Small Scale Industries in Thrust Sectors

- *Interest Subsidy:* In accordance with the priority of developing small-scale industries in the thrust sectors, where working capital is more important than capital cost, the Government will provide interest subsidy at the rate of 5% per annum for 5 years up to a maximum of Rs. 0.5 million (Rs. 5 lakhs) to all industrial units coming up in the State
- *Additional Interest Subsidy:* For industries promoted by Scheduled Tribes/Scheduled Castes, an additional subsidy

at the rate of 2% will be given subject to a maximum of Rs.40,000 per annum

- *Change of Land Use:* The payment of conversion fees for converting the land from agriculture use to industrial use will be waived for tiny and small scale industrial units
- *Technology Upgradation Fund:* The Government will create. a technology Upgradation fund of Rs. 300 million (Rs.30 crores) over the next 5 years to provide financial assistance to small and medium scale industries as interest subsidy against loans taken from banks / financial institutions for technology upgradation
- *Quality Certification:* The Government will encourage small and medium scale industries to obtain ISO 9000, ISO 14000 and similar international certification by meeting 50% of the cost of obtaining such certification subject to a ceiling of Rs.75,000 per unit

Apart from the incentives highlighted above, all industries irrespective of their category will be entitled to the following:

- *Exemption from Entry Tax:* Exemption on entry tax will be extended to all industries including large and medium scale industries. Details of these incentives will be issued separately
- *Payment of Stamp Duty:* All new industries will be exempt from the payment of stamp duty. In addition, new industries will be eligible for a reduction in registration charges to Re.1 per Rs.1 000 while availing financial assistance from banks/financial institutions.
- *Technology Patents:* A facilitation cell will be set up within CSIDC to assist entrepreneurs in matters relating to Patent and Intellectual Property Rights provisions. Industries and R&D institutions in the State will be encouraged to obtain patents -50% of these expenses subject to a maximum of Rs. 0.5 million (Rs. 5 lakhs) will be met by the State Government
- *Additional Incentives:* All new medium and large scale industries where women constitute more than 30% of the

workforce will be given additional incentive equivalent to 10% of the capital investment or Rs. 0.2 million (Rs. 2 lakhs) per annum, whichever is less, for a period of 5 years.

IMPLEMENTATION AND MONITORING

The implementation and review of the industrial policy will be undertaken on a periodic basis in view of the dynamic business environment in the country.

- All concerned departments and institutions shall issue follow-up notifications to give effect to the provisions of this policy within 60 days of the declaration of this policy
- A joint working committee will be immediately constituted with representatives from industry to advice the Government on policy implementation
- SIPB under the chairmanship of the Chief Minister would regularly review the policy and make modifications as may be required from time to time
- A report on the implementation of the policy will be submitted by the Department of Commerce and Industry to the SIPB which will also be made available in the public domain.

Conclusion: The Industrial Policy is intended to set the agenda for achieving measurable goals and targets that the State has set for itself as part of Vision- 2010. These include:

Double the Net State Domestic Product (NSDP): The NSDP (at constant 1993-94 prices) would increase to Rs. 300,710 million by 2009-10 from the current Rs 153,710 (approx.) at a CAGR of 7.75%. This growth in NSDP would increase gradually from 4.2% in 2001-02 to 11.5% by the year 2009-10 in real terms

Redefine Sectoral Composition of NSDP: All the three sectors would contribute to the envisaged growth in NSDP. However, in line with the longer-term developmental priorities of the Vision, the sectoral composition of the economy would undergo changes. At present, the major contributor to NSDP is the primary sector, accounting for 37% of the NSDP. However, by 2010 the tertiary sector would replace the 2000.01 2009.10 primary sector as the major contributor to the economy and would account for 41% of NSDP.

Primary Sector: The contribution of this sector to the NSDP is expected to decrease to about 31% by 2010. This however, does not imply that the thrust on this sector would reduce. It just implies that other sectors would grow at a higher rate over the next 10 years. The growth rate of the primary sector is expected to double in the first 5-6 years, during which time the State would follow a strategy of leveraging on its key strength - natural resources.

Secondary Sector: By 2010, the contribution of the secondary sector to the economy is expected to remain at its current level. Growth in this sector is expected to be fuelled by the growth in the primary sector and through new investments in value added industries.

Tertiary Sector: The tertiary sector comprises transportation, trade, tourism, real estate, banking, etc. The tertiary sector would grow in tandem with the growth in the primary and secondary sectors in the initial years. But, this growth would increase significantly in the later years, by which time the State would have made considerably more progress in terms of building its physical infrastructure.

Increase for Capital Income by Over Rs. 5000. The per capita income would increase from the present value of Rs. 7,072 to Rs.12, 276 in 2010, growing at a CAGR of 6.17%. This is expected to increase over the years as a result of the increase in the rate of growth of NSDP and a reduction in the rate of growth of population.

Annexure—Development Approach and Methodology: The Annexure briefly describes the approach considered and methodology\followed by the State for the development of the Industrial Policy. Development Approach & Methodology

1. Identify engines of growth or thrust areas -thrust areas have been determined based on factors such as current and projected contribution to State Domestic Product,

potential for employment generation, and investment multipliers. Across these thrust industries, emphasis has been on value addition and creation.

2. Determine the tools available with Government to stimulate industrial growth -
   - Measures to implement transparent, business oriented and responsive governance;
   - Budgetary provisions for contribution towards and provision of basic and specialised infrastructure services; and
   - Judicious selection from a range of fiscal incentives available (taxes, capital and interests subsidies, etc.)
3. Apply these tools to thrust industries to achieve strategic objectives—the critical parameters on the basis of which the tools available have been applied to thrust industries include, contributions to the development of physical and social infrastructure, participation in the development of ancillary industries, employment generation, innovation and technology upgradation, and human resource development.

The growth targets defined in Chhattisgarh's Vision 2010 are:

- To attract large investments in core sector and downstream industries;
- To become the power hub of India -by promoting low cost pithead based thermal power plants; and
- To build on locational advantages to develop the State into a regional logistics and transhipment hub.

The State also recognises that these strategic objectives have to be combined with managing complex development challenges, which include:

- Ensuring sustainable utilisation of natural resources;
- Supporting and enhancing indigenous entrepreneurial initiatives and capabilities;
- Building and maintaining basic physical infrastructure;

- Developing and empowering its human resource base;
- Attracting large scale investments, both domestic and international; and
- Strengthening institutional capability for accountability, transparency and efficient delivery of public services.

It is in this context of balancing the need to meet strategic objectives and managing sometimes-conflicting development challenges, that the new industrial policy of the State has been formulated. The policy specifically seeks to define the role of the Government in this critical process of moving forward as a pro-active enabler of industrial development.

A Note on Directed Incentives, Good Governance and Excellent Infrastructure: A large number of reports, including business media reports, evaluate factors that attract investment in States, and describe the importance of infrastructure and hassle free governance, while terming incentive based competition among States as a 'Prisoners' Dilemma' -a race to the bottom.

Especially relevant is the 1998 study on 'Policy Competition among States in India for attracting Direct Investment" by NCAER {National Council for Applied Economic Research). This describes the correlation of investment with infrastructure at 0.6, while the correlation with incentives is only 0.08.

A highly relevant and contemporary study, two months before the creation of Chhattisgarh, is the September 1999 report on "Fiscal Industrial Incentives of the Government of Madhya Pradesh by NIPFP (National Institute for Public Finance and Policy).

This has determined Chhattisgarh's strong bias towards good governance and excellent infrastructure, over and above giving preference to incentives.

GOOD GOVERNANCE AND EXCELLENT INFRASTRUCTURE

Good Governance: The Government of Chhattisgarh is committed to providing a business friendly environment and to minimising rules and procedures that impede efficiency and add to the transaction costs of doing business in the State.

The State will lay emphasis on self-certification, elimination of redundant documentation and approvals, and time based commitments. Accordingly, the existing Statutes (Central and State) will be reviewed and replaced with industry friendly guidelines for doing business in the State. Recommended changes in the Central Statutes will be referred to the Central Government for approval. The process of review and consultation is already underway and will be completed within 90 days. In line with these objectives the Government has already taken initiatives that include:

Administrative Reform

- Under a specific statute, the State Investment Promotion Board (SIPB), to be chaired by the Chief Minister, will be made the single contact point for investment proposals of Rs.200 million (Rs.20 crores) and above. SIPB will provide assistance at pre-investment, investment as welt as post investment stages. SIPB shall, on behalf of investors, obtain all necessary clearances within defined time limits. SIPB shall be assisted by Regional Investment Promotion Committees, to be chaired by suitably senior officials. These Regional Committees, will have overriding powers over most government approvals. They would be the single point of contact for investment proposals below Rs.200 million (Rs.20 crores).
- To reduce the multiplicity of application forms, a combined application form will be introduced, facilitating single point clearances.
- The Government will introduce a comprehensive system of self-certification for the purpose of availing incentives. Certification will be done by a Statutory Auditor. Such self-certification will also be accompanied by a stringent penalty structure, in case of default.
- The Government will update and revise the list of non-polluting industries. The Regional Investment Promotion

Committee will be made responsible for receiving and processing applications for clearances and approvals from the Environment Protection Board.

- For Pollution Control, self-regulatory mechanisms would be promoted and market based instruments to promote voluntary compliance would be introduced.
- The multiplicity of records to be maintained, periodical returns to be filed by industries under various acts/rules, and the existing system of inspection will be rationalised.

Labour Laws : Chhattisgarh has perhaps the most peaceful industrial relations scenario in the country, with the lowest number of mandays lost in industrial disputes. In addition, the time taken for conciliation of industrial disputes is much lower than the national average. This heritage would be promoted in the future as well.

- The Government is undertaking a comprehensive review of all existing labour policies in the context of economic liberalisation. This would be in association with industry and labour representatives. The review will evaluate recent initiatives of some Indian States to streamline the provisions of the Industrial Disputes Act, specifically relating to chapter V-B, and sections 9-A and 25-M
- The State would actively take up with Government of India the issue of small-scale industries employing less than 50 workers to be exempted from the purview of these labour laws
- The Government would encourage introduction of productivity linked wages

Industrial Land Allotment

- Decisions on applications for land allotment / conversion would be made within 30 days. On expiry of 30 days from the date of application for conversion to the appropriate revenue authority, the conversion will be deemed to have taken place. The Regional Investment Promotion Committee will issue a certificate of deemed conversion of land and the necessary entries will be made in the revenue records by the gram panchyats / revenue authorities concerned.

- Regional Investment Promotion Committee will form land banks in each district, and will be authorised to allot up to 5 hectares of Government land for industrial purposes. Government land in excess of 5 hectares will be allotted with the approval of the State Investment Promotion Board.

Excellent Infrastructure: The Government of Chhattisgarh is committed to developing excellent infrastructure for industrial development.

Recognising the critical need for development of infrastructure, the Government has created Chhattisgarh Infrastructure Development Corporation (CIDC) under the chairmanship of the Chief Minister. CIDC has the mandate to catalyse investments for infrastructure development in the State with the participation of the private sector.

CIDC has already prepared a comprehensive Infrastructure Development Action Plan to identify the infrastructure development needs of the State across infrastructure sectors.

Infrastructure Development

- Ensuring good quality-adequate power good roads, transportation and telecom facilities will be the highest priority for the State. Good urban infrastructure for better quality of life will be a major objective.
- The State will take up on a priority basis, the improvement of road linkages within the State by creating two north-south and four east-west high speed road corridors
- Emphasis will be laid on developing rail connectivity to southern Chhattisgarh (Dalli Rajhara -Jagdalpur) to help realise the industrial potential in the region
- Independent Power Producers and State Governments desirous of setting up low cost pit-head based thermal power plants in the State will be encouraged.

- Industrial water has already been earmarked in the existing Water Resources Master Plan. Up to 10% water from new projects will be reserved for industrial use for new as well as existing industries. Industries would be encouraged to set up water harvesting structures on rivers/ streams with necessary approvals.

Industrial Estate Development

- Considering the requirements of the thrust sectors all existing industrial estates will be strengthened and upgraded
- The Government will encourage establishment of Industrial Estates in public- private partnership for which the Government will acquire and make available land
- The Government will contribute 20% towards the cost of development of infrastructure subject to a maximum of Rs. 20 million (Rs.2 crores) in Industrial Estates developed in public-private-partnership
- The Government will promote setting up of Export Promotion Industrial Parks, Gems and Jewellery Parks, Information Technology, Special Economic Zone, and Bio Technology Parks in the private sector. The Government will provide equity support or offer land at concessional rate for these projects
- Operation and maintenance of Industrial Estates developed by the State Government would be handed over to professional management agencies. The Government will allocate a portion of its revenue from the respective Industrial Estates for the purpose of operation and maintenance
- In line with its strategy to promote cluster based industrial development assistance will be provided for establishing common facilities covering quality improvement, technology upgradation, market promotion and technical skills. Financial assistance up to Rs. 20 million (Rs. 2 crores) will be considered per cluster

- Private industrial estates will also be allowed to install Captive Power Plants to generate and distribute power directly within the Industrial Estate

Human Resource Development

- The State Government will constitute a State Vocational Training Council. This council will coordinate the planning and development of the system for vocational and industrial training activities and programmes in all public and private sector-training agencies. This council will be headed by an eminent local industrialist
- The Government will encourage setting up technical institutes in the State by the private sector / business houses, for which land at concessional rates will be provided. Management of Industrial Training Institutes / Polytechnics will be handed over to Industry Associations
- The Government will create a Human Resource Development Fund to encourage direct private sector participation in skill development programmes. Manufacturing companies employing more than 50 workers will be required to contribute 1% of the monthly wage bill to the fund. Manufacturing companies with employees less than 50 but more than 10 will have to contribute 0.5% of the monthly wage bill. To assist these employers, the Government will contribute twice the amount of contribution by the employer. The employer in turn will be eligible to apply for training grants up to three times the contribution to this fund.

DEVELOPMENT STRATEGIES

Chhattisgarh has identified four basic strategies in this Industrial Policy:

Cluster based industrial development;

Good governance and excellent infrastructure;

Improving the competitiveness of small scale industries;

Directed incentives.

Cluster Based Industrial Development

On the basis of its competitive advantages the State has identified five areas of focus. The State would welcome investments in other areas by entrepreneurs, but would concentrate its efforts to provide international cost advantages in thrust sectors.

Good Governance and Excellent Infrastructure

The Government will play a key role to enable public-private-partnership for rapid industrial development and to provide a conducive business environment. The Government's role would include:

- Formulating and implementing stable macro-economic policies;
- Ensuring transparency and accountability in the administering of rules and regulations;
- Enhancing allocations, through budgetary support, borrowings and public-private-partnerships, towards the provision of basic and specialised physical infrastructure especially in industrial parks; and
- Concerted human resource development.

Improving Competitiveness of Small Scale Industries

SSIs have large potential for employment generation and are crucial for economic and social development of the State. SSIs in the State will be developed through pro-active policy initiatives to enhance competitiveness in a market driven economy. This would include initiatives to improve product and service quality, skill development and market access. The policy aims at the long-term sustainable growth of the sector rather than short-term subsistence and on strengthening indigenous entrepreneurial skills.

Directed Incentives

Instead of small incentives spread thinly, the Government would concentrate on the provision of excellent infrastructure.

However, the State does realise the need for encouraging thrust sectors and providing fiscal benefits in the immediate term to attract new industries in these thrust areas. Accordingly, Chhattisgarh would follow a system of directed incentives that help generate investment and employment, enhance competitiveness of indigenous enterprises, and contribute towards the development of physical and social infrastructure.

The specific actions and policy initiatives based on these strategies are outlined in the subsequent sections.

ACTION PLAN: CLUSTER BASED INDUSTRIAL DEVELOPMENT

Cluster Based Industrial Development : For the specific purpose of developing strategic industry clusters, the State has identified the following thrust sectors:

- Agro-based and Forest-based industries
- Agro Processing Units
- Livestock and Livestock Products
- Floriculture
- Fisheries
- Minor Forest Produce processing units
- Medicinal and Herbal products

Mineral based Industries

- Iron and Steel, including downstream industries
- Cement, including downstream industries
- Aluminium, including downstream industries
- Coal based and other chemicals
- Fly Ash based industries
- Gems and Jewellery
- Granite

Traditional Industries

- Handlooms and Handicrafts

Sunrise Industries

- Information Technology
- Bio Technology

Infrastructure Provisioning as Industry

- Power Generation, Transmission, Distribution
- Roads and Transportation
- Urban Infrastructure including development of New Raipur
- Water

The State will also actively promote strategic economic clusters in the following areas:

- Tourism including Eco-Tourism
- Warehousing.

Detailed viability studies will be undertaken in these areas, in collaboration with relevant Industry Associations on the basis of which specific packages will be subsequently announced.

Role of Government : The five thrust sectors would require customised strategies. To facilitate industry clustering, the Government will pursue the following strategies:

- Linkages—all levels of Government will work to develop linkages among the key players in individual clusters.

Programmes and activities of the Government will be aimed at formation of alliances among firms and between firms, and with technical and business support institutions

- Human resource development—the Government will seek to bridge skill gaps by identifying the human resource needs of each sector and accordingly initiating appropriate technical training programmes
- Investments—the Government will focus on attracting external investment by forging partnerships with the private sector and working closely with relevant Industry Associations

Agro-based and Forest-based Industries: The State

recognises the importance of value addition in the primary sector that provides the largest contribution to the State Domestic Product and employs 80% of the State's population. The forward linkages from cultivation to processing will be developed through:

- Industries involved in the processing of food grains, fruits, vegetables, herbal and medicinal plants
- Industries based on livestock processing and fisheries
- Development of specialised industrial estates to provide infrastructure facilities of cold storage, post harvest storage and air freighting of fruits, vegetables and other perishables
- Making available wasteland/degraded land on long-term lease for plantation purposes to encourage forest based industries. In order to promote integrated agro industrial complexes the State Government will allot wasteland up to 500 hectares (in exceptional cases up to 1000 hectares) for such projects, based upon the technical and financial viability of such schemes
- Incorporating special provisions in the Agricultural Land Ceiling Act to encourage Corporate Farming and integrated processing and value-addition units
- Developing Agro Processing Information and Technology Centres in collaboration with institutions such as Confederation of Indian Food Trade and Industry and Central Food Technological Research Institute
- Pro-actively liasing with Financial Institutions to facilitate funding of value added centres for grading, packing, distribution, cold storage, etc.

Mineral based Industries: Chhattisgarh is the richest in terms of mineral potential in the country, with large deposits of Coal, Iron Ore, Bauxite, Gold, Diamond, etc. Instead of exporting minerals, Chhattisgarh would concentrate on processing these minerals to maximise value addition within the State. This sector has immense potential for attracting large investments and generating employment. Accordingly, the Government will take steps to:

- Undertake modern methods of exploration like remote sensing and arrow magnetic surveys to prepare the resource inventory of various minerals across the State
- Prepare zoning atlases of all districts to identify 'Special Mining Zones' for optimum and streamlined mining activities with least disturbance to the ecological balance. An appropriate system will be formulated for obtaining all clearances through a nodal agency under a time bound schedule for undertaking mining activity in these special mining zones
- Forge partnerships with other nations/states for exploration of minerals
- Promote mineral based industries including beneficiation and enrichment of low-grade minerals
- Special focus would be on Iron and Steel, Cement, Aluminium, Coal based chemicals, Fly Ash based industries and granite.
- Establish gems and jewellery park.

Traditional Industries: Product development and marketing efforts for the handicrafts and handloom sector will be strengthened through collaborative efforts with contemporary design centres and export promotion councils.

Sunrise Industries

- *Information Technology:* Chhattisgarh has accorded very high priority to Information Technology (IT). A nodal technical agency called CH/PS (Chhattisgarh Infotech Promotion Society) has been created with a high-level Governing Council chaired by the Chief Minister. The three areas of focus are.
- *Promoting IT Industry:* Setting up a Software Technology Park in Bhilai, the knowledge capital of the State, with 2 MBPS scalable International Gateway Hub. This would be an excellent opportunity for software businesses to locate

in peaceful, software savvy areas that do not have astronomical living costs -Bhilai is 25 km from Raipur and has excellent quality of life.

- *Promoting IT in Governance:* Government-citizen G2C interfaces, as well as Government-Government G2C private investments in both would be encouraged.
- *Promoting IT in Education:* Using static and dynamic networks, training and human resource development would use IT to the utmost. Special focus areas would be Secondary schools, Middle and Primary schools, and Colleges, and private-public-partnerships would be encouraged.
- *Bio-Technology:* The promising field of Biotechnology would be utilised to improve agricultural productivity and agro-processing industry, considering the large primary sector activity in the State.

Infrastructure Provisioning as Industry : The new State offers major opportunities in the industry of infrastructure provisioning as an industry.

- *Power:* Chhattisgarh is poised to emerge as the power hub of India, with its enormous coal reserves and cheapest pithead power generation. The rapid increase in power generation would come about through private investment. The State would encourage such generation in the private sector, and would help in the sale of this power to other States and consumers outside the State. In addition, evacuating this power to deficit States would require large investments, which would be encouraged in the private domain. Distribution of power in select industrial and urban areas would also attract private investment.
- *Roads and Transportation:* Chhattisgarh has decided to develop two North-South road corridors, and four East-West road corridors, of a total length of about 3000 km. This would lead to large investment opportunities in related areas, as also privatising the provisioning of these roads

wherever commercially viable. Bus and Truck transportation would be entirely in the private domain, and big-ticket investment in these areas would be welcomed.

- Urban Infrastructure including development of New Raipur : The State proposes to develop a new Capital, called New Raipur, which would be its largest infrastructure development project. In addition, 6 Municipal Corporations and 20 Municipalities would require upgradation of infrastructure, which would come largely from private investment.
- *Water:* The first private-public partnership in industrial water provisioning has taken place in Chhattisgarh Borai industrial estate in Durg district. The State would encourage private provisioning of infrastructure in industrial, domestic and agricultural water sectors.

TRANSPORT

Roads

Chhattisgarh has coverage of mostly two-lane or one-lane roads which provides connectivity to major cities. Eleven national highways passing through the state which are together 3078.40 km in length.

However, most national highways are in poor condition and provide only two lanes for slow moving traffic. Many national highways are on paper and not fully converted into four-lane highway. This includes 130A New, 130B New, 130C New, 130D New, 149B New, 163A New, 343 New, 930New.. Other national highway includes NH 6, NH 16, NH 43, NH 12A, NH 78, NH 111, NH 200, NH 202, NH 216, NH 217, NH 221, NH30NH 930 NEW. The state highways and major district roads constitute another network of 8,031 km.

Chhattisgarh has one of the lowest densities of National Highway in Central and South India (12.1 km/100,000 population) which is similar to the North Eastern state of Assam.

Rail network

Raipur Railway Station Entrance

Almost the entire railway network spread over the state comes under the geographical jurisdiction of the South East Central Railway Zone of Indian Railways centred around Bilaspur, which is the zonal headquarters of this zone. The main railway junctions are Bilaspur Junction, Durg and Raipur, which is also a starting point of many long distance trains. These three junctions are well-connected to the major cities of India.

The state has the highest freight loading in the country and one-sixth of Indian Railway's revenue comes from Chhattisgarh. The length of rail network in the state is 1,108 km, while a third track has been commissioned between Durg and Raigarh. Construction of some new railway lines are under process. These include Dalli-Rajhara–Jagdalpur rail line, Pendra Road-Gevra Road Rail Line rail line, Raigarh-Mand Colliery to Bhupdeopur rail line and Barwadih-Chirmiri rail line. Freight/ goods trains provide services mostly to coal and iron ore industries in east-west corridor (Mumbai-Howrah route). There is lack of passenger services to north and south of Chhattisgarh. Current train stations are mostly over crowded and not maintained well for passengers.

Rail network expansion

Presently, Chhattisgarh has a 1,187-kilometre-long (738 mi) railway line network, which is less than half of the national average of rail density.

The construction of a new 546-km-long rail network includes the Rajhara-Rowghat rail project, 311km-long east and east-west rail corridors and the 140km-long Rowghat-Jagdalpur rail project.

The Chhattisgarh government has decided to form a joint venture company with the Ministry of Railways for the expansion of railway tracks in the state. The decision to form a joint venture company with the Ministry of Railways was taken during a meeting of the state cabinet chaired by the Chief Minister on 5 February 2016. The state government will have a 51% share and the railways the remaining 49% share.

Major railway heads are Bilaspur, Raipur, Durg, Champa, Raigarh, Rajnandgaon.

Major railway stations of Chhattisgarh

- Bilaspur Junction Railway Station
- Durg Junction Railway Station
- Raipur Junction Railway Station
- Bhatapara Railway Station
- Raigarh Railway Station
- Korba Railway Station
- Champa Junction Railway Station
- Rajnandgaon Railway Station
- Dongargarh Railway Station
- Gevra Road Railway Station
- Pendra Road Railway Station

Air

Swami Vivekananda Airport Raipur

The air infrastructure in Chhattisgarh is small compared to other states. Swami Vivekananda Airport in Raipur is its sole airport with scheduled commercial air services. A massive reduction in sales tax on aviation turbine fuel (ATF) from 25 to 4% in Chhattisgarh in 2003 has contributed to a sharp rise in passenger flow. The passenger flow has increased by 58% between 2011 and November 2012.

Other major areas in the north and south of state, and industrial cities such as Bilaspur, Korba, Raigarh are not served by any airline. The majority of population in these area is not able take advantage of low-cost airlines due to poor road connectivity and high cost of taxi fares. The State Government has signed a MOU with the Airports Authority of India (AAI) in July 2013 to develop Raigarh Airport as the state's second airport for domestic flights.

Other airstrips

- Bilaspur Airport, Bilaspur
- Kodatarai Airport, Raigarh

- Jagdalpur Airport, Jagdalpur
- Nandini Airport, Bhilai
- Baikunth Airstrip, Baikunth
- JSPL's Airstrip, Raigarh
- Ambikapur Airport, Darima, Ambikapur
- Korba Airstrip, Korba
- Agdih Airstrip, Jashpur
- Dondi Airstrip, Dondi, Durg
- Kota Road Airstrip, MohanBhatha, Bilaspur
- Mulmula Airtrip, Mulmula Janjgir-Champa

Proposed airstrips

- Kanker
- Kabirdham
- Surajpur
- Dantewada
- Bijapur
- Korba
- Balrampur
- Rajnandgaon

7

Tourism

TOURISM

Chhattisgarh, situated in the heart of India, is endowed with a rich cultural heritage and attractive natural diversity. The state is full of ancient monuments, rare wildlife, exquisitely carved temples, Buddhist sites, palaces, waterfalls, caves, rock paintings and hill plateaus.

There are many water falls, hot springs, caves, temples, dams and national parks and wildlife sanctuaries in Chhattisgarh.

Tourism in Chhattisgarh refers to tourism in Indian state of Chhattisgarh. It is India's 10th largest state and situated in the heart of India, is endowed with a rich cultural heritage and attractive natural diversity. The state has many ancient monuments, rare wildlife, exquisitely carved temples, Buddhist sites, palaces, water falls, caves, rock paintings and hill plateaus. Most of these sites are untouched and unexplored and offer a unique and alternate experience to tourists, compared to traditional destinations which have become overcrowded. For tourists who are tired of the crowds at major destinations will like the Bastar district, with its unique cultural and ecological identity. The green state of Chhattisgarh has 41.33% of its area under forests and is one of the richest bio-diversity areas in the country.

Waterfalls

View of Chitrakot Falls, Jagdalpur

Beautiful waterfalls in Chhattisgarh are Akuri Nala and Amritdhara falls, Chirimiri is the Jannat Of Chhattisgarh. The Amrit Dhara Waterfall, Koriya, is a natural waterfall which originates from the Hasdeo River. The point where the water falls, there, a cloudy atmosphere is formed all around. The Amrit Dhara waterfall is easily accessible from Koriya and other parts of Chhattisgarh. In addition, there is Gavar Ghat waterfall, Ramdaha Waterfall in Koriya district, Tiger Point Waterfall at Mainpat in Surguja district, and Chitrakot and Tirathgarh waterfalls in Bastar district.

List of Waterfalls of Chhattisgarh

Bastar District

- Chitrakote Falls
- Teerathgarh Falls
- Chitra Dhara
- Tamda Ghumar
- Mendri Ghumar
- Mandwa Waterfalls
- Jhulna Darha
- Chik-Narra
- Shiv-Ganga
- Bhunbhuni

Dantewada District

- Malangir
- Saath-Dhaar
- Fool-paad
- Jhara-lava
- Munga
- Toyer Nala Waterfall
- Dudma Jhodi WF

Jashpur District

- Dangiri
- Ranidah
- Kotebira
- Rajpuri
- Bhringraj
- Gullu
- Churi
- Bane

Korba District

- Damau Dhara
- Deopahrinjnj

Dhamtari District

- Narhara

Kanker District

- Malaj-kudum
- Charre-Marre

Korea District

- Amrit-Dhara
- Ramdah
- Gaurghat Waterfall (Tarra, Sonhat)

Bijapur District

- Lankapalli WF
- Bogtum Waterfall
- Nambi Dhara

Surguja District

- Tiger Falls
- Dev-Pravah

Gariyaband

- Godena Falls
- Deo-Dhara
- Chingra-Pagaar
- Jatmai Falls
- Ghata-rani Falls

Temples

Notable and ancient temples in Chhattisgarh include: Shri Ram Janki Temple at Setganga in Mungeli District, Bhoramdeo temple near Kawardha in Kabirdham district, Rajivlochan temple at Rajim and Champaran in Raipur district, Chandrahasini Devi temple at Chandrapur, Vishnu temple at Janjgir, Damudhara (Rishab Tirth) and Sivarinarayana Laxminarayana temple in Janjgir-Champa district, Bambleshwari Temple at Dongargarh in Rajnandgaon district, Danteshwari Temple in Dantewada district, Deorani-Jethani temple at Tala gram and Mahamaya temple at Ratanpur in Bilaspur district, Laxman temple at Sirpur in Mahasamund district, Uwasaggaharam Parshwa Teerth at Nagpura in Durg district, Pali with Lord Shiva temple and Kharod with Lakshmaneswar temple, Patal Bhairavi temple in outer area of Rajnandgaon. Giraudhpuri is a religious place for the Satnamis. They are the followers of Satnam Panth.

Sirpur is proposed world heritage site and Malhar are of historical significance, as they were visited by Xuanzang, the Chinese historian. Mama- bachha temple at Barsoor.

The hot spring known as Taat Pani, (*taat* - hot, *pani* - water) the hot spring flows in Balrampur district. This hot spring flows throughout the year and is reputed to have medicinal properties due to its high sodium content. National Thermal Power Corporation Limited is developing a geothermal power plant at Taat Pani, which is described as the first geothermal power plant in India.

National parks and wildlife sanctuaries

Achanakmar Wildlife Sanctuary in the Bilaspur district, Gamarda Reserve forest at Sarangarh in the Raigarh district, Indravati National Parkand Kanger Ghati National Park in the Bastar district, Barnawapara Wildlife Sanctuary in the Mahasamund district, Udanti Wildlife Sanctuary in the Raipur district, and Sitanadi Wildlife Sanctuary in the Dhamtari district are good places for eco-tourism.

There is also Guru Ghasidas National Park. The natural beauty of Koriya is known all over India. The place has many dense forests, mountains, rivers and waterfalls, and is known for the rich mineral deposits. Coal is found in abundance in this part of the country. The dense forests present here have a rich wildlife, and the district was where the last known Asiatic cheetah was spotted in the wilderness of India.The climate of Koriya is quite pleasant. The mild summers and cool winters make Koriya a suitable place to visit throughout the year.

List of National Parks

- Kanger Ghati National Park, Bastar District (Area: 200 sq. km)
- Indravati National Park, Bijapur District (Area: 1258 sq. km)
- Guru Ghasi Das National Park, Korea District (Area: 2898.705 sq. km)

List of Sancturies

- Achanakmar, Bilaspur/Mungeli 1975
- Abhay Jain Raipur 1999

- Bhairamgarh, Bijapur 1983
- Barnawapara, Balodabazaar 1976
- Gomarda, Raigarh 1975
- Pamed, Bijapur 1983
- Semarsot. Balrampur 1978
- Sitanadi, Dhamtari 1974
- Udanti, Gariyaband 1972
- Tamor Pingla, Surguja 1978
- Bhoramdeo, Kawardha 2001

Caves and archaeological sites

Gadiya mountain in Kanker district, Kotumsar cave in Bastar district, Kailash gufa in Jashpur district, Ramgarh and Sita Bengra in Surguja district and Singhanpur cave in Raigarh district with pre-historic paintings are well known. There are cave paintings at Ongana and Kabra Pahad near Raigarh, though most of the paintings lie in open and have been over written by graffiti. Archaeological sites worth seeing are Barsoor in Dantewada district, Malhar and Ratanpur in Bilaspur district, Sirpur in Mahasamund district, Koriya in Koriya district and Surguja in Surguja district. A small picnic spot with waterfall on the extremity of Satpura range along with a stone inscription of c. 1st century CE is found at Damau dharain Janjgir-Champa district.

List of some Caves found in Chhattisgarh

Bastar District

- Aranyak Cave Kanger Ghati National Park
- Dandak Cave Kanger Ghati National Park
- Kailash Caves Kanger Ghati National Park
- Devgiri Cave Kanger Ghati National Park
- Jhumar Cave Kanger Ghati National Park
- Kanak Cave Kanger Ghati National Park
- Kotumsar Cave

- Mendhkamaari Cave Kanger Ghati National Park
- Rani Cave Kanger Ghati National Park

Kanker District

- Jogi Cave, Gadiya Mountain Kanker
- Sondayee Cave, Kanker

Jashpur district

- Kailash Cave
- Khudiya Rani Cave

Rajnandgaon district

- Mandipkhol Cave

Bijapur

- Shakal-Narayan Cave, Bijapur
- Shankanpalli Cave, Bijapur
- Usur Cave, Bijapur

Surguja

- Jogi-mara
- Sita-bengra
- Laxman Bengra
- Haathi-pole

Dams

Hasdeo Bango Dam (105 kilometres (65 mi) from Bilaspur), Khudiya Dam in Lormi and Khutaghat Dam (35 kilometres (22 mi) from Bilaspur) in Ratanpur and Gangrel Dam and Murrum Silli Dam in Dhamtari, Kherkatta Reservoir in Pakhanjore are some of the important dams in Chhattisgarh.

TOURS AND TRAVELS

Bhilai : It is famous for Iron & Steel Plant. It is the only steel city of Chhattisgarh State. It is famous for technical tourism. Visitor passes are issued by the P.R.O. Department.

The main places in the Steel Plant are: Coke oven battery, Blast furnace, Rail & Structure Mill, Plate Mill, Wire Rod Mill etc.

Maitribagh: Maitribagh is famous for its garden & is situated under the township of Bhilai. The garden is build by the cooperation of India-Russia Govt. It has a beautiful musical fountain which happens to be the biggest in Asia and it attracts large crowds. It is also famous for its Zoo. Various types of Indian & Foreign animals & birds are kept in this zoo. The zoo also consists lake, toy train and many more.

Deobalod : It is situated about 3 km. from Bhilai & is famous for Oldest Shiv Mandir.

Tandula : It is 60 km. away from the district of Durg. It is famous for Dam on the river Tandula. It is an exciting picnic spot. One can stay here in the rest house of irrigation department.

Dhamdha : It is situated on the Durg-Bemetara road 35 km. from the district of Durg. It is famous for Prachin Kila (Oldest Palace) & Mandir. Lodge & hotel facility are there for the staying of tourist.

Balod : It is situated at 58 km. from the district of Durg. It is famous for Prachin Kila (Oldest Palace), Mandir (Temples) & Sati Chabutra.

Siyadevi : It is around 20 km. (80 Km from Durg city) from balod (Must See Place). This place is famous for Sita Maiya's temple, situated in the heart of greenery of natural jungle. You can find a natural and very beautiful waterfall between (July-Feb.).

Nagpura : It is situated at 2 km. from the district of Durg. It is famous for Jain Temples & Pasharwanath Tirth.

Kharkhara : It is 95 km. away from the district of Durg by road. It is famous for Dam on the river Kharkhara. The total length of the dam is 1128 m.

Culture: The people of Bhilai also have a great tendency towards adopting new trends and life styles. Bhilai thus is multi-cultural for people from all over the world have come and settled in this region. Bhilai's people are also known for their simplicity, kind-heartedness and adaptability. And this is the actual culture of Bhilai.

The people of this region are very fond of colours. The dresses they wear are all colourful. Women too wear sarees with Kardhani. In rural areas women wear mala made of one rupee coins. Though this has gone out of trend these days. The people of this region are also known for creating humour out of language. Comical plays are very popular and are worth watching.

Bhilai is rich in its cultural heritage. Bhilai has its own dance styles, cuisine, music, and traditional folk songs in which sohar song, bihav (marriage) song, and Pathoni songs are very famous. Sohar songs are related to childbirth, Bihav songs are related to marriage celebration.

The main parts of Bihav songs are Chulmati, Telmati, Maymouri, Nahdouri, Parghani, Bhadoni and other songs related to Bhanver, Dowery and Vidai songs. Pathoni songs are related to gouna (departure of bride to bridegroom home). Seasonal Chhattisgarhi folk songs are Fag (Basant Geet), Baramasi (12 months), Sawnahi (in rainy seasons). Festival's related Chhattisgarhi folk songs are Cher-Chera songs (in welcome of new crops, child songs), Dohe of Rout Nacha (Dipawali), Sua songs (Dipawali).

Regional folk songs are Goura songs (worships Shivji & Parvati in Dipawali), Mata Seva songs, Janvara songs, Bhojali songs, Dhankul songs, songs of Nagpanchami. Loriya & playing songs of child are Loriya, Fugdi, Kau-Mau, Chau-Mau, Khuduwa (Kakdi), Dandi Pouha. Karma songs, Danda songs & Dewar songs are most popular of Entertainment songs in Bhilai.

Bhilai is rich in its cultural heritage. Durg has its own dance styles, cuisine, & music. Pandwani the musical narration of the epic Mahabharata, "Raut Nacha" (The folk dance of cowherds) and the Panthi and Soowa dance styles are very popular in the region. Teejan Bai, the Pandwani artist was awarded Padmashree for her contribution to this dance style. Ritu Verma is also a well known name.

People of Durg celebrate marriage and other cultural festivals like Navakhani, Ganga Dushhara, Sarhul Chherka, Dushara, Dipawali, Karma & Kartika.

Tribes: The scheduled tribes, with a population of over fifty seven lakh, constitute 32.5 per cent of the State's population as per the 1991 census. Almost 98.1 per cent of this population lives in the rural areas and only 1.9 per cent in urban Chhattisgarh. Among the larger States in India, Chhattisgarh has the highest percentage of population of people from the scheduled tribes. However, Madhya Pradesh is still the home to the largest population of scheduled tribes in India.

The scheduled tribes are concentrated in the southern, northern and the north-eastern districts of the State.. The highest concentration is in the erstwhile Bastar district. The new district of Dantewara has 79 per cent tribals followed by Bastar (67 per cent) Jashpur (65 per cent), Surguja (57 per cent) and Kanker (56 per cent).

The Gonds at 55.1 per cent form the largest proportion within the tribal population. They are distributed almost equally in the urban and rural areas. The Oraons, the Kawars, the Halbis, the Bharias or Bhumiars, the Bhattras and the Napesias also form a substantial portion of the tribal population. Thirty other scheduled tribes have small population residing in various pockets across Chhattisgarh.

The Gonds are concentrated in the hilly parts of southern Chhattisgarh but are also spread across most districts whereas the Baigas, Bharias, Korwas and Napesias occupy only specific pockets. The Bhattras, Kolams and Rasjas largely live in Bastar and the Kamars in Raipur. The Halba tribe inhabits parts of Bastar, Raipur and Rajnandgaon. The Oraons live in Surguja and Raigarh districts.

There are 9500 villages, or 48 per cent of all inhabited villages, which have more than half their population belonging to the tribal groups. Thirty per cent of all inhabited villages have more than three fourths population from the scheduled tribes. The tribals constitute 100 per cent of the population in 1262, or 6.4 per cent villages.

The districts of Raipur, Durg and Janjgir Chhampa have less than twenty per cent tribals. There are a total of 42 tribes in Chhattisgarh, principal among then being the Gond tribe. Besides, a large population of Kanwar, Brinjhwar, Bhaina, Bhatra, Oraon, Munda, Kamar, Halba, Baiga, Sanwra, Korwa, Bharia, Nageshia, Manghwar, Kharia and Dhanwar tribe are also found in the State.

Economy: Chhattisgarh is rich in forest resources. About 44 per cent of the total area of the State is under forest cover. Chhattisgarh is famous in the entire country for its sal forests. In addition, teak, bamboo, saja, sarai and haldi are also found in large numbers. Tendu leaf, which is used in beedi-making, is the principal forest produce of the State. Chhattisgarh produces a large number of minor forest products as well.

Chhattisgarh has been famous for its rice mills, cement and steel plants. Durg, Raipur, Korba and Bilaspur are the leading districts in the field of industrial development in the State. The Bhilai Steel Plant (BSP) in Durg district happens to be the largest integrated steel plant of the country. The establishment of BSP in the 1950's led to the development of a wide range of industries at Raipur and Bhilai.

Raipur district has got the rare distinction of having the largest number of big and small-scale cement plants. Bilaspur and Durg districts, too, are home to a number of large-scale cement plants. Korba, with a number of power generating units established by NTPC and MPEB, is among the leading power generation centres in the country. Aluminium and explosive plants are also located in Korba district. There are a number of industrial growth centres in the State which host hundreds of industrial units. The principal growth centres in the State are - Urla and Siltara (Raipur); Borai (Durg) and Sirgitti (Bilaspur).

These facilities are now in the developing stage in Chhattisgarh. The total length of rail lines in the State is 1000 kms. The total road length in the State is 32,385 kms. Out of it 21,686 is tarred

INDRAVATI NATIONAL PARK

Indravati National Park is the finest and most famous wildlife parks of Chhattisgarh. Also the only Tiger Reserve in the state, Indravati National Park is located in Dantewada district of Chhattisgarh. The Park derives its name from the Indravati River. With a total area of approximately 2799.08 sq km, Indravati attained the status of a National Park in 1981 and a Tiger Reserve in 1983 under the famous Project Tiger of India to become one of the most famous tiger reserves of India.

The flora in the Indravati National Park is mainly comprises of tropical moist and dry deciduous type with predominance of the Sal, Teak and Bamboo trees. There are also rich patches of excellent grasslands providing much required fodder to Wild buffalos, Chital, Barking Deer, Nilgai, Gaurs and other herbivores of the park. The most commonly found trees in the park are Teak, Lendia, Salai, Mahua, Tendu, Semal, Haldu, Ber and Jamun. The major wildlife in Indravati National Park include the endangered Wild Buffalos, Barasinghas, Tigers, Leopards, Gaurs (Indian Bison), Nilgai, Sambar, Chausingha (four-horned Antelope), Sloth Bear, Dhole (Wild Dog), Striped Hyena, Muntjac, Wild Boar, Flying Squirrel, Porcupine, Pangolins, Monkeys and Langurs among many others.

The commonly found reptiles in the park are Freshwater Crocodile, Monitor Lizard, Indian Chameleon, Common Krait, Indian Rock Python, Cobra and Russell's Viper to name a few. The Park also gives shelter to the large variety of birds of which Hill Maina is the most important species here.

KANGER VALLEY NATIONAL PARK

Located amidst the 34 km long and scenic Kanger Valley, a Biosphere Reserve, Kanger Valley National Park is one of the most beautiful and picturesque national parks of India. The beautiful park is located on the banks of Kholaba River at a distance of about 27 km from Jagdalpur (headquarters of Bastar). Spread over an area of approximately 200 sq km comprising mainly of hilly terrain, the Park derives its name from the Kanger River, which flows throughout its length.

Known for its scenic beauty and the unique and rich biodiversity, Kanger Valley attained the status of a National Park in 1982. Besides wildlife and plants, there are many tourist attractions inside the park such as the Kutamsar Caves, Kailash Caves, Dandak Caves and Tiratgarh Waterfalls. Kanger Dhara and Bhaimsa Dhara (a Crocodile Park) are the two beautiful and exotic picnic resorts in the Park.

The flora in the park chiefly comprises of mixed moist deciduous type of forests with predominance of Sal, Teak and Bamboo trees. In fact, the Kanger Valley is the only region in the Peninsular India where one of the last pockets of virgin and untouched forests still left. Major Wildlife of the Kanger Valley National Park are the Tigers, Leopards, Mouse Deer, Wild Cat, Chital, Sambar, Barking Deer, Jackals, Langurs, Rhesus Macaque, Sloth Bear, Flying Squirrel, Wild Boar, Striped Hyena, Rabbits, Pythons, Cobra, Crocodiles, Monitor Lizards and Snakes to name a few. The avian fauna at the Park includes Hill Myna, Spotted Owlet, Red Jungle Fowls, Racket-tailed Drongos, Peacocks, Parrots, Steppe Eagles, Red Spur Fall, Phakta, Bhura Teeter, Tree Pie and Heron among many others.

SANJAY NATIONAL PARK

Located in Surguja and Koriya districts of Chhattisgarh, Sanjay National Park is one of the most important wildlife sanctuaries in central India. Also known as Ghasi Das National Park (in Chhattisgarh), the sanctuary is famous for its rich and diverse flora and fauna and attained the status of a National Park in 1981. Sanjay National Park covers an area of approximately 2,303 sq km and is well drained by a number of rivers, rivulets and other perennial sources of water, providing enough water supply for the for the wildlife and birds. Sanjay National Park houses a wide variety of wildlife and birds including some of the rare and endangered species and has great potential to emerge as one of the finest wildlife destinations in central India.

The flora in Sanjay National Park chiefly comprises of mixed forests dominated with Sal and extensive patches of Bamboo forests. Other major plants in the sanctuary include Salai, Dhawada (Anogeissus latifolia), Palas (Butea monosperma), Gurajan (Lania choromendelica), Semal, Mahua, Harra, Haldu, Ber and Tendu. The rich and diverse vegetation supports a wide variety of wildlife in the Park.

The major wildlife found in Sanjay National Park includes Tigers, Leopards, Chital, Nilgai, Chinkara, Jackals, Sambar, Four-horned Antelopes, Jungle Cat, Barking Deer, Porcupine, Monkey, Bison, Striped Hyena, Sloth Bear, Wild Dogs, Wild Pigs, Cobra, Monitor Lizards, Python to name a few. Sanjay National Park is also a little paradise for bird lovers and houses wide varieties of avian population with prominent being the Parrots, Peacock, Bulbul, Minivets Orioles, Wagtails, Munias, Blue Kingfisher, Phakta, Ducks, Neelkanth Pigeon, Dabchick, Peafowl, Crimson Breasted Barbet, Teetar, Tree Pie, Racket-tailed Drongos, Egrets, and Herons to name few. A visit to Sanjay National Park promises to be an exciting and rewarding experience for all wildlife enthusiasts and nature lovers.

BARNAWAPARA WILDLIFE SANCTUARY

Located in northern part of Mahasamund district of Chhattisgarh, Barnawapara Wildlife Sanctuary is one of the finest and important wildlife sanctuaries in the region. Established in 1976 under Wildlife Protection Act of 1972, the sanctuary is relatively a small one covering an area of only 245 sq km. The Barnawapara Wildlife Sanctuary is known for its lush green vegetations and unique wildlife.

The flora of Barnawapara Wildlife Sanctuary chiefly comprises of tropical dry deciduous forest with Teak, Sal, Bamboo and Terminalia being the prominent trees. Other major plants found in the sanctuary include Semal, Mahua, Ber and Tendu. The rich and lush vegetation cover supports a wide variety of wildlife in the sanctuary. The major wildlife of the

Barnawapara Sanctuary include Tigers, Sloth Bear, Flying Squirrels, Jackals, Four-horned Antelopes, Leopards, Chinkara, Black Buck, Jungle Cat, Barking Deer, Porcupine, Monkey, Bison, Striped Hyena, Wild Dogs, Chital, Sambar, Nilgai, Gaur, Muntjac, Wild Boar, Cobra, Python to name a few. The sanctuary also has a sizable bird population with prominent being the Parrots, Bulbul, White-rumped Vultures, Green Avadavat, Lesser Kestrels, Peafowl, Wood Peckers, Racket-tailed Drongos, Egrets, and Herons to name few.

SITANANDI WILDLIFE SANCTUARY

Located in Dhamtari district of Chhattisgarh, Sitanadi Wildlife Sanctuary is one of the most famous and important wildlife sanctuaries in central India. Established in 1974 under Wildlife Protection Act of 1972, the sanctuary covers an area of approximately 556 sq km, comprising of highly undulating and hilly terrain with altitudes ranging between 327-736 mts.

The beautiful sanctuary derives its name from the Sitanadi River that originates in the middle of sanctuary and joins Mahanadi River near Deokhut. Sitanadi Wildlife Sanctuary is known for its lush green flora and rich and unique and diverse fauna and has great potential to emerge as one of the finest wildlife destinations in central India.

The flora in Sitanadi Wildlife Sanctuary chiefly comprises of moist peninsular Sal, Teak and Bamboo forests. Other major plants in the sanctuary include Semal, Mahua, Harra, Ber and Tendu.

The rich and lush vegetation cover supports a wide variety of wildlife in the sanctuary. The major wildlife found in Sitanadi Sanctuary include Tigers, Leopards, Flying Squirrels, Jackals, Four-horned Antelopes, Chinkara, Black Buck, Jungle Cat, Barking Deer, Porcupine, Monkey, Bison, Striped Hyena, Sloth Bear, Wild Dogs, Chital, Sambar, Nilgai, Gaur, Muntjac, Wild Boar, Cobra, Python among many others. The sanctuary also has a sizable bird population with prominent being the Parrots, Bulbul, Peafowl, Pheasant, Crimson Breasted Barbet, Teetar, Tree Pie, Racket-tailed Drongos, Egrets, and Herons to name few. Sitanadi Sanctuary is also being prepared to develop it as an important tiger sanctuary in the region.

UDANTI WILDLIFE SANCTUARY

Located in Raipur district of Chhattisgarh, Udanti Wildlife Sanctuary is a small but an important wildlife sanctuary in the region. Established in 1983 under Wildlife Protection Act of 1972, the sanctuary covers an area of approximately 232 sq km. The beautiful sanctuary derives its name from the Udanti River flowing from the west to east covering major part of the sanctuary. Udanti Wildlife Sanctuary is famous for its population of the endangered Wild Buffalos. A large number of man-made tanks have been constructed all across the width and length of the sanctuary.

The flora in Udanti Wildlife Sanctuary chiefly comprises of Tropical Dry Peninsular Sal forests and Southern Tropical Dry Deciduous Mixed Forests. Major flora in the sanctuary comprises of Teak, Sal, Salai, Bamboo, Mahul, Semal, Mahua, Aonwla, Tendu, Harra and Ber among others. The wildlife found in Udanti Sanctuary include Wild Buffalos, Panthers, Tigers, Chital, Four-horned Antelopes, Chinkara, Black Buck, Sambar, Nilgai, Jungle cat, Barking Deer, Sloth bear, Gaur, Wild dog, Porcupine, Monkey, Jackals, Bison, Striped Hyena, Fox, Cobras, Pythons etc. The sanctuary also has a sizable population of birds with prominent being the Parrots, Bulbul, Peafowl, Racket-tailed Drongos, Egrets, Heron, Magpie robin, Lesser whistling Teal, Pintail, Rollers and Herons to name few.

TRIBAL TOURISM

If we talk about tribal tourism, then Chhattisgarh is one of the most fascinating tourist destinations of not only in India but the world. Known for its exceptional scenic beauty and unique and rich cultural heritage, Chhattisgarh has always been synonymous with tribes and tribal culture. Over one third of the state population is of tribes, most of them inhabiting in the thickly forested areas of the famous Bastar region. The tribes of Chhattisgarh are unique in their lifestyles and have beautifully retained their own culture and traditions for centuries. If you are the one who is looking to discover the unique tribal culture of India, then Chhattisgarh offers a perfect destination for you.

Bastar is the largest tribal district of Chhattisgarh with over 70% of its total population comprising of tribals, which is about 26.76% of the total tribal population of Chhattisgarh. There are several tribal castes in Chhattisgarh with Gonds of Bastar being the most prominent among them. The Gond Tribes are well known for their unique Ghotul system of marriages, in all over the world.

Other major tribes of Chhattisgarh region include the Baiga, Korba, Abhuj Maria, Bison Horn Maria, Muria, Halbaa, Bhatra and Dhurvaa tribes. The tribes of Chhattisgarh are known for their unique and distinctive tribal culture and each tribal group has its own distinct culture and enjoys its own unique traditional living styles.

They differ from each other in their costume, eating habits, customs, traditions and even worship different form of god and goddess. Undoubtedly, Chhattisgarh is the most important tribal destination in India and the region has a great potential for tribal tourism.

The tribes of Chhattisgarh region are also known for their passion for dances and music, which are the most important amusements and a part and parcel of their day-today life. The tribal women of the Chhattisgarh region love to adorn themselves with plenty of ornaments made of cowries, beads, shells, bones, feathers, mixed metals, copper and bronze.

The Chhattisgarh tribes are also known for their beautiful arts and crafts. Among festivals, Dusshera is the most important festival of the region but it's different from the north Indian Dusshera. Dusshera Festival of Bastar tribes is celebrated with much enthusiasm in Chhattisgarh every year when all the major tribes of the region gather at the Danteshwari Temple at Dantewada to worship the goddess Danteshwari. Undoubtedly Chhattisgarh is an undiscovered paradise, offering a tourist destination with a difference. Visit Chhattisgarh to see the colourful tribal dances and colourful festivals, which would surely be an exciting and rewarding experience for you on your Chhattisgarh Tour.

ECO TOURISM

Chhattisgarh, the 26th state of the Indian Union, is located in the central part of India. The newly formed Indian state of Chhattisgarh is famous for its enchantingly beautiful natural landscapes, rich cultural heritage and unique tribal populations. With over 44% of its total area under forests, Chhattisgarh is also amongst the greenest states of India. The Chhattisgarh region is known as a great repository of biological diversity. The unique combination of rich cultural heritage and biological diversity makes Chhattisgarh an ideal eco-tourism destination with immense potentials for the growth eco-tourism the region. The Indian Govt. is actively collaborating with the local officials of the state to realize the full potential of eco tourism growth of the region in order to make Chhattisgarh as one of the most important eco-tourism destinations in India.

Chhattisgarh is one of the greenest states of India with over 44 % of its total area under lush forests. The forests of Chhattisgarh are not only known for their diverse flora and fauna but also contain about 88 species of medicinal plants. In addition, Chhattisgarh has also formulated several ecological plans and working in the direction to become the country's first bio-fuel self-reliant state by 2015. And to achieve this goal the green state has devised a plan to plant over 100 million saplings of Jatropa Carcus. Chhattisgarh is also unique in its wildlife population and has 3 National Parks and 11 Wildlife Sanctuaries, housing some of the rare wildlife and bird species. With so much of variety for eco tourism, Chhattisgarh promises to be an ideal holiday destination for nature lovers, wildlife enthusiasts and also for those who want to discover the unique tribal life of the region.

Chhattisgarh has identified some regions with a very high potentiality for eco-tourism. The green state has launched an eco-tourism project covering three potential tourist tracks - Raipur-Turtiria-Sirpur, Bilaspur-Achanakmar and Jagdalpur-Kanger Valley National Park. In addition, a number of herbal gardens and natural health resorts have been created with increased local participation.

The use of ethno-medicine, which has been practiced by aboriginal tribes since centuries, predating even Ayurveda, is also being promoted in Chhattisgarh. The major eco-tourism attractions, which are getting prime attention in Chhattisgarh, include the protection and development of the wildlife areas, camping grounds and trekking facilities. With so many initiatives, Chhattisgarh is destined to become the most favourite eco-tourism destination in India and few among best in the world.

THEATRE

Habib Tanvir—The Making of a Legend: In any culture and in any age, it is rare for a person to become a legend in his or her own lifetime. Yet, judging by the immense enthusiasm and interest with which his productions are received by large audiences in different parts of the country, the 76-year old stalwart of contemporary Indian stage, Habib Tanvir, seems to have already attained this distinction. However, since legends are not born but made, it is instructive to remember that Tanvir's great success and popularity was not given to him on a platter but was earned through a lifetime of serious and sustained effort and struggle.

In popular mind, the name of Habib Tanvir is closely linked to the idea of the folk theatre. However, when he began his career, "folk" had not yet become a major preoccupation in contemporary theatre practice. In fact, he can be regarded as one of the pioneers of the interest in folk forms and traditions of performance. Nonetheless, his approach to folk culture distinguishes itself sharply from that of many others in contemporary theatre. His approach to the folk in particular and his cultural consciousness in general were shaped in the crucible of the left-wing cultural movement -- particularly Indian

People's Theatre Association (IPTA) and Progressive Writers' Association (PWA)—in which Tanvir actively participated during his early, post-university years.

Tanvir traces the genesis of his interest in the folk to his childhood. He was born and brought up in Raipur, which was at that time a small town surrounded by villages on all sides. There was daily and constant interaction between the residents of the town and the village folk. Although his immediate family was town-based, some of his uncles were landowners and visited the countryside often. As a child, he too had several opportunities to visit villages where he listened to the music and songs of the local people. He was so fascinated by these melodies that he even memorised some of them. After finishing school, he was sent to Aligarh Muslim University for his Bachelor's degree. Having completed his studies there, he moved to Bombay in 1945 and immediately joined IPTA and PWA there.

Tanvir's twin interest in poetry and music found its first major expression on stage with Agra Bazar, which he wrote and produced soon after moving to Delhi in 1954. When he arrived in Delhi, and began his career in the theatre, the Capital's stage scene was dominated by amateur and collegiate drama groups which offered English plays in English, or in vernacular translation, to a socially restricted section of the city's anglophone elite.

These groups, as also the NSD a decade later, derived their concept of theatre, their standards of acting, staging, and direction, from the European models of the later 19th and early 20th centuries. There was little effort to link theatre work to the indigenous traditions of performance, or even to say anything of immediate value and interest to an Indian audience. In complete contrast to this, Agra Bazar offered an experience radically different, both in form and content, from anything that the city had ever seen.

The play, as we know, is based on the works and times of a very unusual 18th-century Urdu poet, Nazir Akbarabadi, who not only wrote about ordinary people and their everyday concerns but wrote in a style and idiom which disregarded the orthodox, elitist norms of decorum in poetic idiom and subject matter. Using a mix of educated, middle-class urban actions and more or less illiterate folk and street artists from the village of Okhla, what Tanvir, in a highly interesting (and, for its time, revolutionary) artistic strategy, put on the stage was not the socially and architecturally walled-in space of a private dwelling, but a bazaar—a marketplace with all its noise and bustle, its instances of solidarity and antagonism, and above all, with all its sharp social, economic and cultural polarities.

The play also foregrounds a poetry that takes the ordinary people (their lives, and their everyday struggles) as both its inspiration and its addressee. It uses the example of Nazir's poetry and his plebeian appeal to challenge orthodox, elitist literary canons. What the play thus offers is a joyful celebration of what Mikhail Bakhtin called 'the culture of the marketplace.'

In Agra Bazar, two major emphases that characterise Tanvir's work in the theatre -- one, an artistic and ideological predilection for the plebeian, popular culture; and, two, a penchant for employing music and poetry in plays not as superfluous embellishment but, much like Brecht, as an integral part of the action—had their first and one of the finest expressions.

Soon after this production, Tanvir went to England where he spent over three years studying theatre at the Royal Academy of Dramatic Arts and Bristol Old Vic Theatre School. He also travelled extensively through Europe, watching theatre. He spent about eight months in Berlin in 1956 and saw several recent productions by Bertolt Brecht (who had died that year). This was Tanvir's first encounter with the German playwright-director's work and he was more profoundly influenced by it than by anything that RADA could teach him.

In fact, on returning to India, he quickly began to unlearn much of what he was taught in England—and thus followed a trajectory of development diametrically opposite to that followed by other British-trained Indian directors. Tanvir was now doubly convinced that no truly worthwhile theatre—that is, no socially meaningful and artistically interesting theatre— was possible unless one worked within one's own cultural traditions and context.

The result of this enhanced awareness was, that disregarding the colonial mind-set that dominated the theatre scene at the time, Tanvir began his long quest for an indigenous performance idiom. This quest went through at least two distinct stages before the director arrived at the form and style which is now the hallmark of his work in theatre. His first move was to work with some folk artists of Chhattisgarh and their traditional forms and techniques. His first production, mounted soon after returning from Europe, Mitti ki Gadi (a translation of Shudraka's Mrichchakatikam), included six folk actors from Chhattisgarh in the cast.

Besides, he used the conventions and techniques of the folk stage, thus giving the production a distinctly Indian form and style. The play, which is still revived from time to time (although it is now performed entirely by village actors), is considered by many as one of the best modern renderings of the ancient classic. Mitti ki Gadi convinced Tanvir that the style and techniques of the folk theatre are akin to the ones implied in the dramaturgy of the Sanskrit playwrights. He believes that the theatrical style of the latter can be accessed through folk traditions.

The imaginative flexibility and simplicity with which the classical playwrights establish and shift the time and place of action in a play, Tanvir argues, is found in abundance in our folk performances. Mitti ki Gadi, as well as his recent production of Visakhadatta's Mudrarakshasa, are practical demonstrations of this fact. For example, changes in time and locale in both productions are suggested through dialogues and movements without formally interrupting the performance.

To quote just one instance from Mitti ki Gadi, when a character orders his subordinate to go to the garden and see if there is the body of a woman there, the subordinate simply runs around the stage once and returns with the answer, 'I went to the garden and found that there is a woman's body there.'

Tanvir and his wife Moneeka Misra (herself a theatre person) founded a company of their own in 1959 and called it Naya Theatre. The group produced a number of plays including modern and ancient classics of India and Europe. Although most of these plays were produced with urban actors, Tanvir's interest in the folk traditions and performers had come to stay and continued to grow. However, it was not until the early 1970s that this involvement reached a new and more sustained phase.

At that stage of his career, Tanvir was not entirely satisfied with his work with folk actors. He recognized two 'faults' (as he calls them) in his approach to them. One, he realised that it was not correct to fix the performance rather rigidly in advance by blocking movements and arranging lighting on paper. This, he felt, did not work with the rural artists who could not read or write and could not even remember which way and on what line they should move. The second difficulty was that, by doing plays in Hindi or Hindustani, he was making these actors speak standard Hindi, a language they were not accustomed to. This had the effect of making them act with a severe handicap and thus of inhibiting the full and free expression of their creativity in performance.

Conscious of these faults, Tanvir began to rid his style of work of them. He started using the method of improvisations. He also allowed the folk actors to speak in their native Chhattisgarhi dialect. The years 1970-73 were an exploratory phase for him. During this period, he worked intensively with rural performers in their native language and style of performance. He allowed them to do their own traditional pieces mostly in their own way, merely editing and touching them up here and there to make them more stageworthy. During this period he tried many things, from temple rituals to stock skits and pandavani.

The second significant breakthrough came during a nacha

workshop that Tanvir conducted in Raipur in 1972. In addition to several observers from the urban centres of Raipur, Delhi and Calcutta, more than a hundred folk artists of the region participated in the month-long exercise. During the workshop, three different traditional comedies from the stock nacha repertoire were selected and more or less dovetailed into one another to make one compact, full length play. A few short scenes were improvised and inserted to link them up into one story. A number of songs, which had never before been brought on the stage were also included after appropriate editing. The production which was thus created was called Gaon ka Naam Sasural, Mor Naam Damaad, an almost wholly improvised and delightful stage play.

The play was a significant turning point in Tanvir's development. With this production, which was a great success not only in Chhattisgarh but also in Delhi, he had broken new ground. He felt that he had found the form and style that he had been searching for ever since his arrival on the theatre scene as a director in the 1950's. After the 1973 workshop, it became easier for him to go on with the construction and casting of a play through improvisations—a method that he continues to use to this day. By the time he produced his masterpiece, Charandas Chor (1975), that evergreen darling of theatregoers throughout the country, the form and style of his theatre had reached its perfection.

Tanvir's Naya Theatre works almost exclusively with folk actors. However, even his occasional productions with urban actors and for groups other than Naya Theatre -- such as, Dushman (Gorky's Enemies) for the NSD Repertory or Jisne Lahore Nai Dekhya Wo Jamyai Nai (Asghar Wajahat) for the Sri Ram Centre Repertory—are marked by the style that he has developed through his work with the folk artists. Nonetheless, the theatre that Tanvir had developed was not a "folk theatre" in the strictest sense of the term. He is a conscious and highly sophisticated urban artist with a modern outlook, sensibility and a strong sense of history and politics. His interest in folk culture and his decision to work with and in terms of traditional styles of performance was itself an ideological choice as much as an aesthetic one, whether Tanvir himself was fully conscious of it as such or not.

There is a close connection between his predilection for popular traditions and his left-wing disposition. His involvement with the left-wing cultural movement, an association which he maintains (no matter how loosely) to this day, already meant a commitment to the common people and their causes. His work in the theatre, in style as well as in content, reflects this commitment and can be seen as part of a larger (socialist) project of empowerment of the people.

Tanvir's fascination with the "folk" is not motivated by a revivalist or an antiquarian impulse. It is based, instead, on an awareness of the tremendous creative possibilities and artistic energies inherent in these traditions. He does not hesitate to borrow themes, techniques, and music from them, but he also desists from the impossible task of trying to resurrect old traditions in their original form and also from presenting them as stuffed museum pieces. Notwithstanding a popular misconception, his theatre does not belong within any one form or tradition in its entirety or purity.

In fact, as he is quick to point out, he has not been "running after" folk forms as such at all but only after folk performers who brought their own forms and styles with them. The performance style of his actors is, no doubt, rooted in their traditional nacha background, but his plays are not authentic nacha productions. For one thing, while the number of actual actors in a nacha play is usually restricted to two or three, the rest being stop-gap singers and dancers, Tanvir's production involve a full cast of actors, some of whom also sing and dance. More significantly, his plays have a structural coherence and complexity which one does not usually associate with the "simple" form of the nacha.

Another important difference is that while in the nacha songs and dances are used largely as autonomous musical interludes, in Tanvir's plays they are neither purely ornamental in function nor are they formally autonomous units inserted into a loose collection of separate skits. On the contrary, they are closely woven into the fabric of the action and function as an important part of the total thematic and artistic structure of the play. v

In other words, Tanvir does not romanticise the 'folk' uncritically and ahistorically. He is aware of their historical and cognitive limitations and does not hesitate to intervene in them and allow his own modern consciousness and political understanding to interact with the traditional energies and skills of his performers. His project, from the beginning of his career, has been to harness elements of folk traditions as a vehicle and make them yield new, contemporary meanings, and to produce a theatre which has a touch of the soil about it.

This rich interaction between Tanvir's urban, modern consciousness and the folk styles and forms is perhaps best exemplified by the songs in his plays. Tanvir's excellent adaptations of A Midsummer's Night Dream (Kamdeo Ka Apna, Basant Ritu Ka Sapna) and The Good Woman of Szechwan (Shaajapur ki Shantibai) could not be possible without this interaction.

In these plays, he has worked close to the original text and written songs which reproduce the rich imagery and humour of Shakespeare's poetry and the complex ideas of Brecht. Despite this fidelity to the original texts, not only has Tanvir given his poetic compositions the authenticity and freshness of the original but has also fitted his words to native folk tunes with remarkable ease and skill.

One of the most outstanding examples of this kind of interaction is Tanvir's Dekh Rahe Hain Nain, based on a story by Stephen Zweig, in which he has successfully represented a complex theme without compromising the vitality and creativity of his folk actors.

It was the moral dilemma embodied in the protagonist, a courageous warrior, who is tormented by the guilt of having to kill his own brother, which had attracted Tanvir to Zweig's story. However, in writing the play, he went beyond the story and invented new events, situations, characters and added dimensions and nuances which significantly enriched the story and made it more poignantly relevant for us today.

The result is a play that traverses a complex gamut of motifs from the abstract, almost metaphysical, quest for inner peace to the concrete, material problems of the ordinary people in wake of a war, economic inflation and political corruption; from an idealist impulse towards renunciation of political power and towards an absolute solitude to an urgent sense of the necessity to get involved with others for a shared endeavour to change the world.

Tanvir is quite careful not to create a hierarchy by privileging, in any absolute and extrinsic way, his own educated consciousness as poet-cum-playwright-cum-director over the unschooled creativity of his actors. In his work, the two usually meet and interpenetrate, as it were, as equal partners in a collective, collaborative endeavour in which each gives and takes from, and thus enriches, the other.

An excellent example of this non-exploitative approach is the way Tanvir fits and blends his poetry with the traditional folk and tribal music, allowing the former to retain its own imaginative and rhetorical power and socio-political import, but without in any way devaluing or destroying the latter. Yet another example can be seen in the way he allows his actors and their skills to be foregrounded by eschewing all temptations to use elaborate stage design and complicated lighting.

Thus in contrast to the fashionable, folksy kind of drama on the one hand and the revivalist and archaic kind of 'traditional' theatre on the other, Tanvir's theatre offers an incisive blend of tradition and modernity, folk creativity and skills on the one hand and modern critical consciousness on the other. It is this rich as well as enriching blend which makes his work so unique and memorable.

8

Population and Religion

POPULATION OF CHHATTISGARH

Chhattisgarh is a state in the central piece of India and it infers 36 fortresses. It is the tenth biggest state in the country with an area of (52,199 sq mi). With a population of around 25.5 million as indicated by 2011, the state is the seventeenth most-populated state of the nation. It is a wellspring of power and steel for India, having 15% of the total steel made in India. It is one of the fastest growing states in the nation.

The state was formed on 1 November 2000 by partitioning 16 Chhattisgarhi-speaking southeastern region of Madhya Pradesh. Raipur was made the capital. Being another state when contrasted with MP, it has been growing at a sound rate. Additionally, one of the finest cricket stadium in India is built in Raipur and it has hosted several IPL matches as well.

Population Of Chhattisgarh In 2018

Chhattisgarh is fundamentally a provincial state with just 20% of its population living in urban regions. A vast group of Bengalis has existed here since the time of the British Raj. They are connected with education, industry and administrations.

Talking about population, in order to check out the population of Chhattisgarh in 2018, we need to have a look at the population of the past 5 years. They are as per the following:

1. 2013 – 26.7 Million
2. 2014 – 27 Million
3. 2015 – 27.9 Million
4. 2016 – 28.2 Million
5. 2017 – 28.84 Million

Predicting the 2018 population of Chhattisgarh is not easy but we can get the idea after analysing the population from the year 2013 – 17. As we have seen that every year the population increases by approximate 0.428 Million people. Hence, the population of Chhattisgarh in 2018 is forecast to be 28.84 Million + 0.428 Million = 29.268 Million. So, the population of Chhattisgarh in the year 2018 as per estimated data is 29.268 Million.

Chhattisgarh Population 2018 –29.268 Million. (estimated).

Demography Of Chhattisgarh:

As demonstrated by the 2011 assessment, the 93.2% of the population took after Hinduism, while 2% followed Islam, 1% Christianity and some of them having Buddhism, Jainism or diverse religions. Sarnaism is the indigenous religion that is followed by the tribes of Chhattisgarh.

It has a high female-male sex extent and it positions at the fifth among various states of India. Regardless of the way that this proportion is little when compared with other various states, it is phenomenal in India in light of the way that Chhattisgarh is the tenth biggest state in the country. The official vernacular is Hindi and is utilized by non-provincial population of the state. Chhattisgarhi, a language of Hindi tongue, is spoken and grasped by the prevailing part of people in Chhattisgarh.

Population Density And Growth Of Chhattisgarh:

The population density of the state is 189 persons per square kilometre. The total population growth in this decade was 22.61% while in previously it was 18.06%. The number of occupants in Chhattisgarh shapes 2.11 percent of India in 2011. In 2001, the figure was around 2.03 percent. Concerning population growth, the state has assumed control over its mother province of Madhya Pradesh.

Facts About Chhattisgarh:

1. With the arrival of the British in 1845, Raipur grabbed significance instead of the Capital Ratanpur.
2. In terms of area, Chhattisgarh is the ninth biggest state and as far as population it is the seventeenth state of the nation.
3. The town of Sirpur on the Mahanadi River is home to the red-piece Laxman Temple, lit up with carvings from Indian folklore.
4. It is surrounded by Jharkhand to the south and Orissa in the east side.
5. During old times, the area was known as Dakshin-Kausal.

POPULATION POLICY

Preamble: The Chhattisgarh State Integrated Health and Population Policy 2006 reiterates the commitment of the State to promote health for all and to provide quality health care services, especially to those in remote and difficult areas. The Policy aims at sustainable human development by ensuring that every citizen has adequate access to basic essentials of life, reducing socioeconomic disparities, improving the quality of life and stabilising the population. Securing the rights of disadvantaged and marginalised groups would be given the highest priority with the aim of eliminating discrimination and responding to the aspirations of the people, so that they can successfully contribute to national reconstruction and social change. Women's empowerment and gender equity would be one of the cornerstones of this policy.

To achieve the goals of National Population Policy 2000 and National Health Policy 2002, the Chhattisgarh Integrated Health and Population Policy takes a holistic view of population stabilisation and improving reproductive and child health services with special attention to decentralised governance. Towards this end the Policy will strengthen the Panchayati Raj Institutions (PRIs) and build its capacities to fulfil this role.

The Chhattisgarh State Integrated Health and Population Policy recognises the pivotal contribution of socio-economic determinants of health. It understands the need for basing health policy on a comprehensive health care approach which integrates issues related to the social determinants with measures for improving health care services. Achieving health equity as part of building a more equitable society would therefore be a major goal of this policy.

The National Rural Health Mission (NRHM) 2005 with its stated goal—"to promote equity, efficiency, quality and accountability of public health services through community driven approaches, decentralisation and improving local governance" has brought back the primacy of Health for All and comprehensive primary health care and provides a platform to foster desired inter-sectoral coordination that is essential to address social determinants and improved health care services in an integrated fashion.

The Chhattisgarh State Integrated Health and Population Policy would be consistent with separate policies that may be formulated for related social sectors and these policies read together would constitute the charter of social development for the people of the state.

Vision: The Chhattisgarh Government commits itself to achieving the highest attainable level of physical, mental and social health through processes that shall empower local communities and be affordable to the State and its citizens, be equitable and gender sensitive and which would reduce poverty in the State. Universal access to comprehensive quality primary health care with adequate referral linkages would be the key strategy through which this vision would be realised.

This is already enshrined in the State's Vision 2020 document. The State shall respond to the health needs of the people and will be guided by principles of transparency, accountability and community participation involving stakeholders from the public, private and non-government organizations to create a society enjoying healthy productive lives in harmony with their social responsibilities and contributing to a national resurgence.

The State is committed to achieving population stabilisation, through a life cycle approach by promoting informed choice, empowering women and communities and paying special attention to reproductive and child health issues of disadvantaged populations living in remote areas.

STRATEGIC DIRECTIONS

Decentralised Planning and Implementation: Panchayati Raj Institutions (Repeated) are an important means to decentralise planning and implementation in the context of National Population Policy 2000 and National Health Policy 2002. To realise their potential, administrative and financial powers would be delegated to these local self government institutions. Representative sub committees in each tier of the Panchayati Raj system will be formed to play an active role in planning and monitoring programme implementation.

These committees would be statutory committees and would act for the health sector as well as for allied social sectors taken together, thus creating an institutional framework for convergence. By providing for special representation of elected women, community level women activists like Mitanins and for representation of community based organization or any other forms of women movements, participation of women in decision making and mainstreaming of gender concerns would be ensured.

The Panchayat Health Committees would also coordinate with state departments and with local community based women's organisations like Self Help Groups to ensure that there are hamlet level health committees, trained community health activists (Mitanin) and peer educators available in every habitation. Periodic training programmes would be institutionalised for both elected PRI members and its administrative and technical support staff.

Institutional mechanisms for PRIs to access technical assistance for planning and programme management would be put in place. The performance of Panchayats would be measured on a set of indicators, called a Health and Human Development Index and this would be periodically published.

This would enable correction of uneven development between Panchayats and within Panchayats by funnelling resources to the Panchayats and sections performing poorly. With growth of capabilities with institutional technical assistance and democratisation with adequate transfer of powers, PRIs especially at the block and district level would be given control over all the health facilities and functionaries in their areas. The state is committed to this goal.

Community Participation: Health should not be a commodity to be consumed or a desirable set of practices imposed by a benevolent state on a passive beneficiary. Health should be produced and sustained at the level of the family as community and it requires not only community participation but adequate community control over the processes that generate health. Towards this end the State Government will develop mechanisms to involve communities in problem identification, planning, implementing and monitoring of health care programmes.

When choosing community representatives for participation in various aspects, the State would be sensitive to socio-cultural, economic, geographical and gender differences. Community initiatives and collective local action would be promoted to address a number of issues that are best addressed locally by people acting together - for example in the control of vector borne diseases, or in the promotion of sanitation. For effective community participation a number of local institutional arrangements would be promoted in the form of village health committees, self help groups, youth clubs and other spontaneous forms of community based organizations.

Providing the nodal point for these community efforts at the level of the habitation and village would be a number of trained and sensitised volunteers and peripheral government functionaries the most important of these being the Mitanins, the Anganwadi worker, the village nurse (multi-purpose health worker) and the primary school teacher.

At the State, district and block level a number of non-governmental organisations would play a major role in ensuring community participation and in promoting the concerns of marginalised sections and regions. These organisations will identify unserved and underserved areas for primary health care services including reproductive health and prepare plans to provide need based, culturally appropriate, and people centred quality care which is responsive to people's felt needs as well. They would work under the guidance of both PRIs and the State government to ensure the successful implementation of these plans.

Comprehensive Primary Health Care: A commitment to comprehensive primary health care would be a commitment to ensuring universal access to promotive, preventive, curative and rehabilitative health care linked together with good referral systems which is responsive to the health needs and aspirations of the people at that given level of social and economic development. It also implies a commitment to processes such as equitable distribution, community participation, intersectoral coordination, the use of appropriate technologies - all of which are essential to achieve these objectives.

With respect to curative care services, comprehensive primary health care in the context of Chhattisgarh would mean, at the least, access to basic 10 to 15 essential drugs and a trained health volunteer in every habitation, access to a trained nurse at the village level, access to a medical curative facility with about 30 to 50 drugs within an hour and access to a centre providing hospitalisation and basic emergency care - the first referral level, within two hours using a readily accessible transport.

The Government shall notify the actual package of services that would be guaranteed in each facility from the health sub centre, the primary health centre, the community health centre or first referral unit and the district hospital and the secondary referral centre. This package which shall be comprehensive, covering communicable and non communicable diseases and would be upgraded annually to reflect acceptable standards of care. Similarly in preventive care the State would define the minimum guarantees in terms of access to food, drinking water and sanitation, elementary education and health education, safe working and living standards and minimum environmental quality standards. Promotion of healthy life style and protection from harmful practices, especially tobacco, liquor and other addictions would also be important components of comprehensive health care.

Equity in Health Care: Further the goal of the State, is not only to achieve adequate status of health for the State as a whole but also to ensure health equity - so that in all crucial indicators of health (like IMR, MMR, disease prevalence rates) and in all crucial health service indicators (like doctor population ratio, or hospital bed population ratio or immunisation ratio, or access to maternal care indicators etc.) there are no significant difference between different economic or social groups.

This in turn commits the Government to taking affirmative action, so that groups which are currently more disadvantaged receive proportionately higher allocation of resources and services, enabling them to close the gap and reach the State averages.

The concept of equity will encompass a wide number of parameters which include economic class, gender, marginalisation by community, by religion, by region, or by criteria of vulnerability like - age groups (old, very young, adolescent) homeless, migrants, urban slum dwellers, commercial sex workers, children without adult protection, physically and mentally challenged and destitutes.

One of the greatest challenges facing the State would be of gender equity. Though relative to other states Chhattisgarh shows a better gender equity situation, it has been noted with concern that the sex ratio in the 0 to 6 age group is declining. Addressing this requires not only enforcement of the PNDT Act but better access to social services for the girl child and a determined campaign against son preference in communities. The past bias towards focusing on some aspects of reproductive health like fertility control has been replaced by a more comprehensive understanding of reproductive health, where reproductive health is seen as a subset of the larger agenda of women's health issues. While the State will endeavour to provide the highest quality of reproductive health as part of a life cycle approach, it would recognise that addressing gender inequities in health care, requires mainstreaming gender concerns in all aspects of health care management. The State would also strengthen and facilitate the emergence and growth of women's participation in decision making and leadership, and promote collective action by women so that women's health care becomes part of a process for women's empowerment.

A majority of health care providers in the State are women and this trend is likely to grow. Women today serve as health volunteers, as midwives and as nurses and increasingly they would be part of the workforce as technicians, pharmacists and doctors. These trends would be encouraged and the needs and concerns of women health care providers would be built into health workforce management policies.

Innovative, flexible, collaborative approaches will be adopted for meeting the health needs of the vulnerable groups. Recognising the high levels of motivation needed to address these vulnerable groups, the State shall seek active partnership with non governmental organisations to reach out to these sections and promote policies so that such groups have a conducive environment to renew themselves and their commitment and extend the services to vulnerable groups on a sustainable basis.

The State will allocate resources for geriatric health care to improve the health status of the elderly by integrating health services for the elderly with primary health care. The State will also promote research and facilitate the establishment of appropriate geriatric health care facilities.

Quality and Standards of Care: Standards and Quality of care parameters will be developed for the different levels of health care for ensuring health outcomes and patient satisfaction. These standards would be developed in consultation with health professionals, public health experts and informed public opinion. The standards would be periodically upgraded to keep abreast of the best practices in national and international areas. These standards would include standard clinical management protocols with rational use of drugs and diagnostics for all categories of health care providers and continuing medical education aimed to ensure that such protocols are adequately taught to the health care providers.

In public health institutions, hospital management committees assisted by technical assistance agencies would ensure that these qualities of care standards are achieved. Systems of accreditation will validate these achievements and convey them into the public domain. Hospital management committees will be provided with the necessary resources, powers and technical assistance to achieve these standards. Similar standards of care would be ensured in large private commercial centre in health care and in the not-for-profit sector as well.

In the private sector a system of voluntary accreditation will facilitate a constant enhancement of quality of care, while a well enforced regulatory mechanism will ensure that basic minimum quality in terms of costs of care, appropriateness and effectiveness of care and ethics of care are guaranteed to the public.

Supplementary mechanisms to ensure quality of care would be a well publicised citizen's charter, and adequate mechanisms of social audit, community monitoring and statutory grievance redressal mechanisms. Appropriate legislation to guarantee and make these above means into health rights would be adopted.

Behaviour Change Communication: The goal of the

strategy is to encourage individuals, families and communities to make informed decisions concerning health care through programmes of health communication, which facilitate behaviour change. Towards this end the State has adopted a Behaviour Change Communication (also known as IEC) strategy and an implementation framework. This framework prioritises the use of interpersonal communication with suitable aids, the use of locally appropriate print media and local cultural art forms especially in the 'kalajatha' format, as main vehicles of effective communication. Electronic media, both radio based and television would also be needed to promote societal change with regard to behaviour norms on health. The content of all BCC programmes would be appropriate to local contexts and audience groups, with careful normative research and evaluation studies. There will be a need to engage a wide variety of communicators beyond the staff of the public health system to make BCC programmes more effective.

Greater dialogue on issues of health between individuals, within families and communities will be needed to promote societal change with regard to behavioural norms on health and particularly on reproductive and child health. The cornerstone of this would be better quality of interpersonal communication between trained health volunteers and health care providers and the families they serve. There will be a critical need for capacity building at all levels to undertake these newly defined tasks and enhance the image of health functionaries.

Districts will become the natural focus for convergence of government and non government efforts for BCC through participatory planning and programme implementation.

Intersectoral Coordination

Intersectoral coordination is essential to ensure that many of the social determinants of health are addressed adequately. Priority areas for such coordination are nutrition and food supply, water and sanitation, and poverty alleviation programmes. The PRI and their statutory social sector sub-committees would be the main institutional framework for intersectoral coordination.

Coordination would include planning job responsibilities and functioning at the village level such that each of the functionaries assist each other in reaching the common goals. The health sector staff, the Mitanins, the panchayat functionaries, primary school teachers and Anganwadi workers will be entrusted with various individual and joint responsibilities in integrated service delivery. The Panchayats will involve civil society in monitoring the availability, access and affordability of services and supplies. Coordination will also ensure adequate registration at the village and panchayat level, of births, deaths, marriages and pregnancies. There would be a joint assessment of progress on different parameters and joint action plans to ensure that progress is accelerated.

DEMOGRAPHICS

Chhattisgarh has an urban population of 23.4 %(around 5.1 million people in 2011) residing in urban areas. According to a report by the government of India, at least 34% are Scheduled Tribes, 12% are Scheduled Castes and over 50% belong to the official list of Other Backward Classes. The plains are numerically dominated by castes such as Teli, Satnami and Kurmi; while forest areas are mainly occupied by tribes such as Gond, Halbi, Halba and Kamar/Bujia and Oraon. A large community of Bengalis has existed in major cities since the times of the British Raj. They are associated with education, industry and services.

Religion

Religion in Chhattisgarh (2011)

Hinduism (93.25%)

Islam (2.01%)

Christianity (1.92%)

Sikhism (0.27%)

Buddhism (0.27%)

Jainism (0.24%)

Sarnaism or not religious (3.01%)

According to the 2011 census, 93.25% of Chhattisgarh's population practised Hinduism, while 2% followed Islam, 1.92% followed Christianity and smaller number followed Buddhism, Sikhism, Jainism or other religions. Sarnaism is the indigenous religion followed by the indigenous tribes of the state.

Witchcraft

To bring about social reforms and with a view to discourage undesirable social practices, Chhattisgarh government has enacted the Chhattisgarh Tonhi Atyachar (Niwaran) Act, 2005 against witchery. Much has to be done on the issue of law enforcement by judicial authorities to protect women in this regard, bringing such persecution to an end. Some sections of tribal population of Chhattisgarh state believe in witchcraft. Women are believed to have access to supernatural forces and are accused of being witches (*tonhi*) often to settle personal scores. As of 2010, they are still hounded out of villages on the basis of flimsy accusations by male village sorcerers paid to do so by villagers with personal agendas, such as property and goods acquisition. According to National Geographic Channel's investigations, those accused are fortunate if they are only verbally bullied and shunned or exiled from their village.

Social Mission Against Blind Faith

Religious persecution

According to the Christian organisation Release International, several Christians in Chhattisgarh have been attacked and killed by Hindu nationalists.

Lachhu Kashap was killed and his brother, Pastor Shuduru Kashap beaten in Mandala, and several other Christians have been beaten by mobs of up to fifty people.

When Chhattisgarh separated from Madhya Pradesh in 2000 it inherited anti-conversion laws which were further tightened in 2007.

Those wishing to convert to Christianity need to submit an official affidavit, leading to an official police investigation into their reasons for converting. Punishment for contravening the regulations can be up to three years' prison or fines of up to 20,000 rupees.

Language

The official languages of the state are Chhattisgarhi & Hindi. Chhattisgarhi is spoken and understood by the majority of people in Chhattisgarh. Among other languages, Odia is widely spoken by a significant number of Odia population in the eastern part of the state. Marathi and Telugu are also spoken in parts of Chhattisgarh. Chhattisgarhi was known as "Khaltahi" to the surrounding hill-people and as "Laria" to Odia speakers.

In addition to Chhattisgarhi, there are several other languages spoken by the tribal people of the Bastar region, geographically equivalent to the former Bastar state, like Halbi, Gondi and Bhatri.

Status of women

Chhattisgarh has a high female-male sex ratio (991) ranking at the fifth position among other states of India. Although this ratio is small compared to other states, it is unique in India because Chhattisgarh is the 10th-largest state in India.

Adivasi woman and child

The gender ratio (number of females per 1,000 males) has been steadily declining over 20th century in Chhattisgarh. But it is conspicuous that Chhattisgarh always had a better female-to-male ratio compared with national average.

Young women in Chhattisgarh

Probably, such social composition also results in some customs and cultural practices that seem unique to Chhattisgarh: The regional variants are common in India's diverse cultural pattern.

Rural women, although poor, are independent, better organised, socially outspoken. According to another local custom, women can choose to terminate a marriage relationship through a custom called *chudi pahanana*, if she desires. Most of the old temples and shrines here are related to 'women power' (e.g., Shabari, Mahamaya, Danteshwari) and the existence of these temples gives insight into historical and current social fabric of this state. However, a mention of these progressive local customs in no way suggests that the ideology of female subservience does not exist in Chhattisgarh. On the contrary, the male authority and dominance is seen quite clearly in the social and cultural life.

Detailed information on aspects of women's status in Chhattisgarh can be found in 'A situational analysis of women and girls in Chhattisgarh' prepared in 2004 by the National Commission of Women, a statutory body belonging to government of India.

Adivasi woman at Farasgaon Market

Natives of Kamar Tribe

9

Art, Architecture, Fair and Festivals

FESTIVALS OF CHHATTISGARH

- Bastar Dussehra/ Durga Puja
- Bastar Lokotsav
- Madai Festival
- Rajim Kumbh Mela
- Pakhanjore Mela (Nara Narayan Mela)
- Lata mangeshkar sang a song for Chhattisgarhi film Bhakla of Dhriti pati sarkar.
- Mohmd Rafi sang a song for Chhattisgarhi film. He had also sung songs for various Chhattisgarhi films like Ghardwaar, Kahi Debe Sandes, Punni Ke Chanda, etc.

Theatre

Theater is known as *Gammat* in Chhattisgarh. Pandavani is one of the lyrical forms of this theatre. Several acclaimed plays of Habib Tanvir, such as *Charandas Chor*, are variations of Chhattisgarhi theatre.

Film industry

Chhollywood is Chhattisgarh's film industries. Every year many Chhattisgarhi film produced by local producers.

Natya Samaroh by IPTA

Traditional food

The State of Chhattisgarh is known as the rice bowl of India and has a rich tradition of food culture.

Red Velvet Mite is used as Medicine in Traditional Healing of Chhattisgarh

Bastar Dassera

Bastar Dassera is the region's most important festival, and all the tribes participate in the 10-day event. The tribals celebrate Dassera as a congregation of Devi Maoli, and all her sisters.

Hundreds of priests bring flower-bedecked local deities to the Danteshwari temple in Jagdalpur, arriving with all pomp and show. Bastar Dassera is believed to have been started, in the 15th century, by Maharaj Purushottam Deo, the fourth Kakatiya ruler.

Bastar Lokotsav

This fortnight-long tourism event, organized to coincide with Bastar Dassera , showcases the best of Bastar. It takes place every year after the monsoons, when the forests and waterfalls are at their best. Tribal handicrafts can be bought directly from artisans. A folk arts festival of tribal dances and music, Bastar Parab, is organized in Jagdalpur.

Madai Festival

This tribal festival is celebrated by the tribes of Kanker and Bastar regions, to worship the local Goddess. The Goddess is taken all through the Kanker, Bastar and Dantewada regions from December to March each year. In December, celebrations start in Bastar to honour the Goddess Kesharpal Kesharpalin Devi. In January, the people of Kanker, Charama and Kurna celebrate the festival. In February the festival goes back to Bastar and Cheri-Chher-Kin is honoured this time. Towards the end of February, the festival goes to Antagarh, Narayanpur and Bhanupratappur. In March it goes to Kondagaon, Keshkal and Bhopalpattanam. It is held in a big ground, so that thousands of people can attend the ceremony, which starts with a procession of the local Goddess, followed by worship of the same, culminating in cultural programs, dancing and lots of good food.

Hareli

Celebrated in the month of 'Shravan', Hareli is a symbol of agricultural prosperity. Farmers worship farm tools and cows on this occasion. They place branches and leaves of 'Bhelwa' (a tree resembling cashew tree) in the fields and pray for good harvest. People also hang small Neem branches at the main entrance of houses on this occasion to prevent occurrence of seasonal diseases.

Pola

Pola follows Hareli. It is celebrated by worshipping bullocks. Children play with idols of Nandi bull (the vehicle of Lord Shiva) made of clay and fitted with clay wheels. A bull race is a major event of the festival.

BhagOdia Festival is a popular festival among Bhil tribes of the region and Bhagoradev or the God of dance is worshipped on this occasion.

Kajari Festival is another important festival of Chhattisgarh region, which falls on the same day as Raksha Bandhan that is on the Shravan Purnima.

Hariyali, Kora, Navakhani and Cherta Festivals are also important agricultural festivals of Chhattisgarh.

Chhattisgarh also organizes many colorful fairs in different towns and cities of the state, all round the year. Rajim Lochan Mahotsav held every year from 16th February till 1st March is celebrated with great fanfare. Bhoramdeo Mahotsav (last week of March), Chakradhar Festival (September or October), Goncha Festival (July), Narayanpur Mela (last week of February) and Sheorinarayan Fair (February) are other widely celebrated and most enjoyed fairs and festivals of Chhattisgarh.

KAJARI FESTIVAL

Introduction to the Kajari Festival: In this land of variety and diversity, fairs and festivals are celebrated with a great deal of brilliance and grandness. The young state of Chhattisgarh is no exception. The Kajari Festival is an important festival in Chhattisgarh and it is of particular relevance to the farmers of the state.

Description of the Kajari Festival: The Kajari Festival is particularly important to the farmers because it heralds the beginning of the sowing season for wheat and barley. It is time to bid adieu to the monsoons and start the preparations for a fresh harvest. These religious minded farmers therefore seek the blessings of Goddess Bhagwati so that they may have a better crop the following year. The customs and rituals that are associated with the Kajari Festival are performed only by women who are blessed with a son. On the day of the Shravan Shukla Navami, the women folk go to the agricultural fields and collect earth in leaf cups. Barley is sown in these cups.

The cups are then kept in a dark room. The rooms are kept clean. The walls and floors are washed with cow dung and mud. Special care is taken to see that neither sunlight nor air penetrates into the room. The floors are also beautifully decorated with designs drawn with rice solution. Some of the staple designs that ornament the floor are figures of a house, a child in cradle, a mongoose and a woman with a pitcher. At the end of it all, the cup is religiously worshipped.

This worship is religiously repeated for seven days till Kajari Purnima or full Moon Day. All these days they continuously pray for the well being of their husband, children and for a good harvest. The celebrations reach its height on the evening of Kajari Purnima. Women observe fast from the morning. Then they carry the cup in their heads in a procession to a nearby pond or water body to immerse it. Time for celebrating the Kajari Festival in Chhattisgarh

The celebrations of the Kajari Festival begin on the ninth day after the Shravan Amavasya. The month of Shravan in the Hindu calendar corresponds to the months of July and August in the Gregorian calendar. This ninth day is referred to as the Kajari Navami or Shravan Shukla Navami. Beginning on the Kajari Navami, the festival continues till the Kajari Purnima or the full moon day. This festival coincides with yet another festival, the Raksha Bandhan.

BHAGORIYA FESTIVAL

Introduction to the Bhagoriya Festival: India's richness lies in its diversity. The multi hued culture of this nation is best manifested in the fairs and festivals that it celebrates with a great deal of ceremonial elegance and splendour. The state of Chhattisgarh is populated by a large number of tribals and their unique culture is also reflected in the festivals that they celebrate with pomp and enthusiasm. The Bhagoriya festival is a festival of the Bhil tribe and is celebrated in the Jhabua district of Chhattisgarh.

Description of the Bhagoriya Festival: The literal meaning of the term Bhagoriya is elopers. Are you wondering why it has been named so? Then get prepared for a real surprise. The most striking characteristic of this festival is that here one is officially given the permission to elope with one's lover. You have to apply gulal on the girl you have liked and if she reciprocates you are at complete liberty to elope with her.

You can also offer her a betel leaf as an expression of your love. If she accepts the token you can rest assure that she has agreed to your proposal and is equally keen on spending the rest of her life with you. Then you can follow the tradition which has been so long followed and run away with your beloved. The marriage will be eventually solemnized.

On the occasion of this festival, Bhagoradev or the God of Dancing is worshipped religiously by the people of the Bhil community. The eldest member of the village supervises over the ceremony. Sweets are offered to the god and later these are distributed amongst the members of the tribe.

The fun is indeed unlimited. Everybody dances to the beat of the drums and the thalis. There is joyousness in the atmosphere and notes of Shahnai and Bansuri fill the air. You will also start tapping your foot and crave to be a part and parcel of this merriment.

Time for celebrating the Bhagoriya Festival: The festival is held just a week before the festival of Holi. Holi is generally celebrated in the month of March and this festival precedes it a week ahead.

CHAKRADHAR FESTIVAL

Introduction to the Chakradhar Festival: The town of Raigarh in Chhattisgarh has carved a niche for itself in the cultural scenario of the country. Several distinguished Kathak

Dancers and Classical Musicians were born on this soil. Mentions worthy among them are Shree Firtu Maharaj and Vijaya Sharma and most importantly Maharaja Chakradhar Singh in whose memory the Chakradhar Festival is held in Chhattisgarh. Maharaja Chakradhar Singh was the former king of Raigarh. He was also a great patron of music and dance. He could play the tabla and was a skilled dancer as well. In addition to that he wrote many books on music. The Chakradhar Samaraho in Raigarh is in honour and remembrance of this great man whose contribution is valued to this day.

Description of the Chakradhar Festival: The Chakradhar Festival is a result of the initiative taken by the Ustad Allaudin Khan Sangeet Academy and the Chakradhar Lalit Kala Kendra, two institutes dedicated to the promotion of music.

Each year, dancers and musicians from different parts of the country come to this Musical Festival in Chhattisgarh to display their talents. It is a wonderful opportunity for them to uphold their endowments. A visit to the Chakradhar Festival in Chhattisgarh will give you the wonderful opportunity to witness the programmes of several jewels at the same time. They all possess exceptional calibre and that is well manifested in their performances. Chhattisgarh Festivals like these reflect the rich cultural heritage of our country.

Folk artistes are also an integral part of this Musical Festival held in Chhattisgarh. The functions include memorable performances by the folk artistes as well. It would be no exaggeration to say that you will remain fastened to your seats when you watch the shows. They are thoroughly enjoyable and enthralling. You will be absorbed and transferred to a totally different world of dance and music. One's interest in the field of performing arts will be all the more roused after a visit to the Chakradhar Festival in Chhattisgarh.

Time for Celebrating the Chakradhar Festival: The Chakradhar Festival is celebrated each year at the time of Ganesh Chaturthi. The Hindu calendar is followed while fixing the date of this musical festival. It roughly corresponds to the months of September or October according to the Gregorian calendar.

GONCHA FESTIVAL

Introduction to the Goncha Festival: The newly found state of Chhattisgarh has a fairly large tribal population. These tribes have a distinctive cultural entity of their own. Their unique culture is best manifested in the festivals that they celebrate with a great deal of pomp and grandeur.

The Goncha Festival in Chhattisgarh is one such tribal festival that is marked by a lot of joy and merry making. It also showcases the inimitable tribal culture. If you can visit the district of Bastar in Chhattisgarh at the time of the Goncha Festival you will get the unique privilege to be a part of the festival that is truly one of its kind.

Description of the Goncha Festival: The Goncha Festival is also popularly known as the Chariot Festival probably because it is celebrated at a time when the Hindus celebrate Rath Yatra. The vigorous and enthusiastic enjoyment that marks the Goncha Festival in Chhattisgarh is remarkable. The zest and hearty spirit of the tribals from different parts of Bastar who participate in this festival is incredible.

There are several customs that are associated with this Chhattisgarh Festival. Goncha is actually a kind of fruit. The tribal people make a pistol using tukki or bamboo. As is evident, it is just a mock weapon that is constructed by them to follow the tradition of the tribe. The fruit Goncha is likewise used as a bullet.

They use the pistol and the bullet, actually a bamboo stick cut in the shape of a pistol and a fruit to strike each other. The intention is not to hurt each other but to just be a part of a mock encounter.

It is a source of unlimited joy for them. They find it very thrilling and exciting. The fervour and gusto of the people of Chhattisgarh at the time of celebrating this festival is admirable.

The celebration of Festivals like these brings to the forefront the ethnicity of this part of the country.

Time for Celebrating the Goncha Festival: The Goncha Festival is celebrated according to the Hindu calendar at the time of Rath Yatra. It generally falls in the month of July according to the Gregorian calendar. If you visit the state of Chhattisgarh at the time of the Goncha Festival, you can be a part of the festivities.

NARAYANPUR MELA

Introduction to the Narayanpur Mela: Festivals such as the Narayanpur Mela in Chhattisgarh reveal a lot about the way of living of the tribals in Chhattisgarh. The religious festivals of the Hindus, Muslims and Christians are celebrated with a great deal of joyous enthusiasm in the state of Chhattisgarh. The Festivals associated with these festivals also serve as the meeting ground of a large number of people.

However the greatest attraction is the fairs and festivals of the tribal community. The tribes living in Chhattisgarh have a distinctive lifestyle of their own and all of us are curious to know about it. A visit to the fairs and festivals in Chhattisgarh will make us familiar with their unique culture. This is because the fairs and festivals are probably the best expressions of their inimitable culture.

Description of the Narayanpur Mela: The Narayanpur Festival is celebrated in the Bastar region of Chhattisgarh. The Bastar district has a sizeable tribal population and they celebrate this festival with a lot of happiness and exuberance. The term Mela literally means fair but the Narayanpur Mela is not a fair but a festival.

On the occasion of this Chhattisgarh festival, the tribal people follow several traditions and customs. They worship the tribal deities. After worshipping their deities with a lot of devotion, they engage themselves in unrestrained merry making. The gaiety of the tribals knows no bounds. Several sessions of drinking are an integral part of the festivities.

All of us are probably well versed with the fact that collective dancing is an essential part of tribal culture. When they celebrate the Narayanpur Mela, their rhythmic dancing to the notes of fabulous drum music is simply a treat to watch. Dancing together without any restrain or reserve is a way of manifesting their joy and elation. Cheerful freewheeling marks this Chhattisgarh Festival and provides valuable insight into the ethnic way of living of these colourful people.

Time for Celebrating the Narayanpur Mela: The Narayanpur Mela is held in the last week of February every year with a lot of merriment

BHORAMDEO MAHOTSAV FESTIVAL

Introduction to the Bhoramdeo Mahotsav Festival: The enamoring state of Chattisgarh celebrates all its festivals with a great deal of fanfare. The Bhoramdeo Mahotsav Festival is no exception. This festival attracts a large number of people not only from the rest of India but also from different parts of the world.

Description of the Bhoramdeo Mahotsav Festival: This festival is celebrated within the premises of the Bhoramdeo temples located at a distance of about 135 km from Raipur. The famous king Ramachandra of the Nag dynasty who married Princess Ambika Devi of the Haiya dynasty is credited with the construction of this temple. The temple is reflective of remarkable architectural dexterity. It is of great relevance to historians and archaeologist's.

The impressive and magnificent temple complex bustles with a lot of activity when the Bhoramdeo Mahotsav is organized. It is indeed a beautiful sight to behold. The vibrant people clad in colourful attires witness this architectural marvel and take part in all the activities that take place.

The Bhoramdeo temples have rightfully received the epithet of Khajuraho of Chattisgarh and if you visit it when the Bhoramdeo Mahotsav is held you are sure to be fascinated.

Time for Celebrating the Bhoramdeo Mahotsav Festival: This festival is celebrated each year in the last week of the month of March. It is best for you to plan your visit to Chattisgarh when you the Bhoramdeo Mahotsav Festival is celebrated.

DUSSEHRA FESTIVAL

Introduction to the Dussehra Festival: Chhattisgarh - a state located in the heart of incredible India is inhabited by a sizeable tribal population. These tribal people have a very unique cultural heritage of their own. They celebrate all their festivals with a great deal of ardour and enthusiasm. The festival of Dussehra is celebrated throughout the country but there is a distinctive difference in the way it is celebrated here. It is marked with the same degree of forever and enthusiasm but it is celebrated for totally different reasons. The return of Lord Rama from his exile to his homeland of Ayodhya is not related to Dussehra in Chhattisgarh in any way.

Description of the Dussehra Festival: Dussehra in Chhattisgarh is celebrated in honour of Sri Danteshwari Mai. She is highly revered and respected by the tribals. According to local legend she safeguarded the Bastar king from the attackers and gave him protection in the forests. As a mark of their gratitude, the tribals still owe their allegiance to her.

The deities from far flung tribal villages are brought to the Temple of Goddesses Danteshwari in Jagdalpur on this day. Jagdalpur is the district capital of Bastar and stands witness to a lot of festivities on the occasion of Dussehra.

There are several other customs also that are associated with Dussehra in Chhattisgarh. The day begins with a worship ceremony at the Kacchhingudi temple. The presiding deity of the temple is placed in a "rath" and all the devotees lend a hand to the rope when the rath is pulled akin to the celebrations in Puri on the occasion of Rath Yatra. In fact the chariot is also made by the Saoras of Orissa.

It is also customary to choose a young girl from the weaver community and place her on a swing of thorns. The girl does not get injured in spite of that and this is supposed to be because of the grace of God. This is considered a very good sign and indicates the goddesses' approval of the festivities.

The joy and mirth of these simple tribal people is indeed unlimited. They enjoy themselves thoroughly. It is a time when they get to meet each other and be a part of all the merry making. At Gole Bazaar, the shops are crowded and they display various handicrafts item. So do try and get a taste of the pomp and pageantry at the time of Dussehra.

Time for Celebrating the Dussehra Festival: The Dussehra festival is celebrated mostly in the month of October or November.

HARIYALI, KORA, NAVAKHANI AND CHERTA FESTIVALS

Introduction to the Hariyali, Kora, Navakhani and Cherta Festivals: The colourful state of Chhattisgarh with a sizeable tribal population celebrates all its festival with a great deal of joy and fervour.

The Hariyali, Kora, Navakhani and Cherta Festivals are different festivals which are celebrated at different points of time. They are referred to collectively because all of these are agricultural festivals.

Agriculture is the backbone of the Indian economy and the state of Chhattisgarh is no exception. Even they are extremely dependant on cultivation for their living. The sowing of new seeds, the reaping of crops, the rich and bountiful harvest—for the people of Chhattisgarh each is an event that is to be celebrated joyously.

So they rejoice whole heartedly on practically all the occasions that are related to agriculture.

Description of the Hariyali, Kora, Navakhani and Cherta Festivals: The Hariyali, Kora and Navakhani Festivals are celebrated when the new crops are gleaned. It is a mark of thanksgiving to the lord for bestowing them with plenty. It is a token of their gratitude as well as a sign of their joy. After the hard work of so many days, their efforts have finally paid off and so they are elated. The term Navakhani literally means eating of the new crop. They consume the grains themselves and offer it along with liquor to their forefathers.

The grains are the fruits of their toils. They want to share their success with their predecessors who have blessed them and this small gesture is perhaps the best way to show their thankfulness. Even when the Cherta Festival is celebrated, the people consume pulse which is their agricultural product. They too remember their ancestors on this auspicious day and raw urda pulse is offered to them as well.

Time for Celebrating the Hariyali, Kora, Navakhani and Cherta Festivals: The Hariyali, Kora, Navakhani and Cherta Festivals in Chhattisgarh are celebrated at various times of the year. The first two Festivals are celebrated in the month of September. The festival of Navakhani is celebrated just in the next month that is in October. January is the month for celebrating the festival of Cherta.

MADAI FESTIVAL

Introduction to the Madai Festival: The state of Chhattisgarh has managed to retain its natural beauty and its old world charm. There is a mysterious aspect to it probably because of the extensive dark forests and the large number of tribal people who inhabit these forests. Little disturbed by the vagaries of modern civilization, these tribal people have a unique culture of their own. One of the old tribal communities in Chhattisgarh is the Gond community. The Madai Festival is celebrated by people belonging to the Gond community with a lot of interest and excitement.

Description of the Madai Festival: The most important feature of the festival is that it is always celebrated in a large ground where it is possible to have a large gathering. After all it is on the occasion of Madai festival that relatives from far and wide come together to laugh, to make merry and to share the joys.

There are several customs which are observed when the Festival of Madai is celebrated. A goat is sacrificed in honour of the tribal gods. This ritual takes place beneath a sacred tree. Then amidst the beating of drums and bells, the goat is taken around the whole village.

A procession of the local gods in which a large number of tribal people participate is the initiation ceremony of the festival. They devotedly offer their prayers and then all the fun and frolic starts.

A large number of shops and eateries are set up on the occasion of the Madai Festival. Many a times, people purchase salt and cooking oil which will last them a year from these shops. You also get to see remarkable examples of the craftsmanship of these tribals often displayed in the shops.

Many cultural programmes are also arranged in the large grounds. There is so much of cheerfulness in the air. The air reverberates with the sound of tribal music and many of them dance to the tunes of these rhythms. Your evenings will surely be very enjoyable because of the memorable performances that they put up.

At night also the merry making continues in full vigore. The men consume intoxicating drinks and dance to the tribal tunes. The sight of this unrestrained merry making is very enjoyable and it is difficult to resist the desire to be one of them and participate in the revelry. The ambience is very cheerful indeed.

Time for Celebrating the Madai Festival: Interestingly the Madai festival is celebrated at different times in different places. The people of Bastar celebrate Madai in the month of December and surely this is the place to be if you want to witness the celebrations of the Madai Festival. The people of Kanker, Charama and Kurna celebrate it in the very next month of January. In the beginning of the month of February, this festival is celebrated once again in the Bastar district and at the end of this month it is time for the people of Antagarh, Narayanpur and Bhanupratappur to rejoice. At last in the month of March it is the turn of the people of Kondagaon, Keshkal and Bhopalpattanam to be a part of the Madai festival.

FAIRS AND FESTIVALS IN CHHATTISGARH

India is a land of rich and varied cultural heritage. The multihued culture of India is best manifested in the various festivals that are celebrated with a great deal of pomp and grandeur throughout the country. The state of Chhattisgarh is no exception.

This colorful state located in central India is bestowed with a lot of natural beauty. The tribals form a major part of the population in this state. The Fairs and Festivals in Chhattisgarh give you the unique opportunity to have a first hand experience of the tribal culture of the state.

Different Fairs and Festivals in Chhattisgarh

Of all the Fairs and Festivals in Chhattisgarh, Dussehra is celebrated with greatest ostentation and ceremony. It is rather interesting to know that Dussehra in Chhattisgarh is celebrated for totally different reasons. While the rest of India burns the effigy of Ravana on the occasion of Dussehra, in Chhattisgarh it is celebrated in honor of Goddess Danteshwari. The tribals participate and bring their deities from the villages to the Temple of Goddess Danteshwari in Jagdalpur.

Unrestrained merry making characterizes the Fairs and Festivals of Chhattisgarh. Rajim Lochan Mahotsav is a fair which lasts for 15 days. A large number of people participate in this colorful carnival. It is a time for all to come together, to exchange greetings, to buy various products that reflect the dexterity of Chhattisgarh craftsmen.

There are several other Fairs and festivals which are celebrated with a great deal of joy.

10

Education

EDUCATION

According to the census of 2011, Chhattisgarh's literacy, the most basic indicator of education was at 71.04 per cent. Female literacy is at 60.59 per cent.

Chhattisgarh is one of the newest states of India. Formed in the end of the year 2000, the Chhattisgarh government is still ill equipped and does not possess the resources required for the overall development of a good education system. However it is due to the constant efforts by the government authorities that the Chhattisgarh education system has recorded an impressive literacy rate of 77.86% for males and 52.40% for females.

The average rate of literacy in Chhattisgarh stands at 65.18% as per the census report prepared in the year 2001. The central and state government establishment has taken steps to promote children's and women's education in Chhattisgarh. Raipur, the capital of this Central Indian state, is also the education hub of Chhattisgarh. Today, resident and non-resident students seek education in Chhattisgarh.

Education System in Chhattisgarh

The education system in Chhattisgarh lacks in basic infrastructure and amenities. But there are quite a few schools and colleges in the state that impart quality education. Hindi is generally used by teachers as the medium of instruction in both schools and colleges of Chhattisgarh. But with demand for English growing, institutes are also trying to incorporate this universally accepted language in their teaching programs.

Absolute literates and literacy rate

Data from Census of India, 2011.

Description	2001 census	2011 census
Total	20,833,803	25,540,196
Male	10,474,218	12,827,915
Female	10,359,585	12,712,281
% Total	64.66	71.04
% Male	77.38	81.45
% Female	55.85	60.59

Education in Chhattisgarh

One of the newly formed states in India, Chhattisgarh covers an area of 135,194 km. It was recognized as a state on 1 November 2000. The education scenario in Chhattisgarh is not very remarkable as it lacks proper educational infrastructure. However, the state government has launched several programs for enhancing the academic scenario of the state.

The overall growth in the literacy rate has been possible due to the persistent efforts of the state government. According to the 2001 census report, Chhattisgarh had a literacy rate of 65.18% which included male and female literacy rate of 77.86% and 52.40% respectively. Special importance is given to the education of women and students belonging to the underprivileged section of the society. The capital city Raipur is the main center of higher education in Chhattisgarh. It houses some of the most important departments of education in the state.

School education

Most of the children in the state generally attend 3 years of

Montessori school before joining 1st standard in the school. The schools in Chhattisgarh follow the same 10+2 pattern of education like the other union territories and states in India. One can come across both private and state-run schools in Chhattisgarh.

The government run schools are mostly affiliated to the Chhattisgarh Board of Secondary Education. Students can also join schools affiliated to the Central Board of Secondary Education (CBSE) or Council for the Indian School Certificate Examination (CISCE).

In the state-run schools Hindi is generally the medium of instruction while English is preferred by most of the private schools. New Life English School Jankpur, Jain International School, Adarsh Vidya Mandir, Gyanganga Educational Academy, Delhi Public School, Kaanger Valley Academy, Bhartiya Sanskriti Higher Secondary School and Salem English School are some of the popular schools in Chhattisgarh. Under Raipur District total 508 including RMSA school .Dr. R. Bambra is deo raipur

HIGHER EDUCATION

Technical education

Most of the colleges and institutions in the state are affiliated to any of these government recognized universities. The colleges in Chhattisgarh offer various courses in architecture, engineering.

Medical education

Most of the colleges and institutions in the state are affiliated to any of these government recognized universities. The colleges in Chhattisgarh offer various courses in biotechnology, dental science, law, hotel management, medical, physiotherapy, mass communication, nursing, veterinary science and management.

Education

Project Description: Nanhi Kali is a joint initiative of KC

Mahindra Educational Trust and Naandi Foundations. The project is aimed at reducing the drop outrates of girl children from Govt. Schools.

Even though parents send their girls to school for the first few years, soon they take them out of the schools with the view that their education would not be beneficial to the family. Nanhi Kali's objective is to keep them in the school longer by paying for their educational costs.

Purpose / Goals: Ensure that the sponsored girl children get atleast 12 years of school education. Bring about a change in the parents view that the education of the girl child is equally important. In Chattisgarh, Naandi/KCMET are working with the Govt. to support the education of Girl children by paying for their educational costs.

Organization Description: Naandi Foundation is a not-for-profit registered Trust working in the areas of Education, Health and Livelihood since 1998. Our Board is chaired by Dr. Anji Reddy of Dr. Reddy's Laboratories Ltd. and includes eminent personalities like Mr. Anand Mahindra of Mahindra & Mahindra, Mr. Ramalinga Raju of Satyam Computers, Mr. KS Raju of Nagarjuna Group and Dr. Isher Judge Ahluwalia, noted economist.

The K. C. Mahindra Education Trust was formed by late Mr. K.C. Mahindra in the year 1953, with an objective to promote education. It is a registered public charitable Trust chaired by Mr. Keshub Mahindra, Chairman of M&M and other trustees include Mr. Anand Mahindra, Vice Chairman & MD of Mahindra & Mahindra and Mr. Bharat Doshi, Executive Director of M&M. The K.C. Mahindra Education Trust has undertaken a number of education initiatives, which has made a difference in the lives of deserving students.

According to the census of 1991, literacy the most basic indicator of education, was 42.9 percent. This is marginally less than the literacy rate of 44.7 percent for undivided Madhya Pradesh. Female literacy is very low at 27.5 percent, especially rural female literacy, which is at 21 percent.

Literacy in Chhattisgarh in 1991

Area	*All*	*Male*	*Female*
Chhattisgarh	42.9 %	58.1 %	27.5 %
Rural	36.7 %	52.4 %	21.0 %
Urban	71.4 %	82.7 %	58.9 %

Source : Primary Census Abstract, Census of India 1991, Registrar General of India.

The low level of literacy, especially amongst women, Scheduled Castes and Scheduled Tribes is a cause for concern. The literacy rate amongst the Scheduled Tribes was 39 percent in 1991 and 27 percent amongst the scheduled tribes.

The general enrolment and access to primary schools in the undivided Madhya Pradesh, including areas of Chhattisgarh has received a tremendous boost in the last decade with increased availability of functional primary schools and the starting of the Education Guarantee Scheme.

Bibliography

Bhargav Arun: *Rural Marketing and Agribusiness in India*, Surendra, Delhi, 2010.

Brijesh Mishra: *Glimpses of Social Welfare in India : Problems and Perspectives*, ABD Pub, Delhi, 2006.

Chaturvedi, Pratima : *Social Work : Theories and Practices,* Book Enclave, Delhi, 2005.

Clough, Richard: *Construction Project Management in Rural India*, New York, John Wiley & Son, 2000.

Dak, T.M.: *Women and Work in Panchayati Raj*, Delhi, Discovery, 1988.

Downs, Anthony: *An Economic Theory of Democracy,* New York, Harper and Row, 1957.

Ehrenberg, Ronald: *Modern Labor Economics,* Harper Collins, 1994.

Evenett, S. and B. Hoekman: *The WTO and Government Procurement,* Northampton, Edward Elgar, 2006.

Hallgren, M. H., & McAdams, A. K.: *The Economic Efficiency of Internet Public Goods*, Massachusetts, MIT Press, 1997.

Harrigan, K. R.: *Strategies for Declining Businesses*. Lexington, MA: Heath, 1980

Hart, Oliver: *Firms, Contracts, and Financial Structure,* Clarendon Press, Oxford, 1995.

Hausman, D. M.: *The Inexact and Separate Science of Economics*, Cambridge, Cambridge University Press, 1992.

Hayek, F. A. *Individualism and Economic Order*, The University of Chicago Press, Chicago, 1948.

Huang, Chi-fu: *Foundations of Financial Economics,* Prentice-Hall, 1988.

Hunt, E. K. *History of Economic Thought, A Critical Perspective,* New York, HarperCollins, 1992.

Jack Kemp: *A Monetary Agenda for the World Economy,* Boston, Quantum, 1984.

Jain S.C. *: New Trends in Rural Marketing*, RBSA Pub, Delhi, 2011.

Kalika Prasad Tiwari: *Foundations of Ancient Indian Culture*, Pointer Publishers, Delhi, 2001.

Kamble, N. D.: *Deprived Castes and their Struggle for Equality*, Ashish Publishing House, New Delhi, 1983.

Karmarkar, D.: *Sankara's Advaita*, Karnatak University, Dharwar, 1976.

Kelly, F. P.: *Charging and Accounting for Bursty Connections*, Massachusetts, MIT Press, 1997.

Kieve, L.: *Urban Land Economics*, London, MacMillan Press, 1977.

Kumari, R. : *Women-Headed Households in Rural India,* New Delhi, Radiant Publishing, 1989.

Levinson, D.: *Family Violence in Cross Cultural Perspective*, Newbury Park, Sage, 1989.

Mayer, A.: *Caste in an Indian Village: Change and Continuity 1954-1992*, Delhi, OUP, 1996.

Metcalf, Thomas R.: *Modern India: An Interpretive Anthology*, London, Macmillan, 1971.

Minakshi, C.: *Administration and Social Life under the Pallavas*, Madras, University of Madras, 1977.

Misra, Satya Swarup: *The Aryan Problem: A Linguistic Approach*, Munshiram Manoharlal, New Delhi, 1992.

Parel , J.: *Hind Swaraj or Indian Home Rule*, Cambridge University Press, 1925.

Ram, Jagivan: *Caste Challenge in India*, New Delhi, Vision Books, 1980.

Richard Davis: *Lives of Indian Images,* Princeton Univ. Press. Princeton, 1997.

Roubos- Bennett, M. : *Redefining Disasters: A Decade of Counter Disaster Planning,* State Library of New South Wales, Sydney, 1996.

Index

❑❑❑